THE AGE OF ACCESS: INFORMATION TECHNOLOGY
AND SOCIAL REVOLUTION

CROOM HELM INFORMATION TECHNOLOGY SERIES
Edited by P.J. Hills, University of Cambridge

COMMUNICATION AND PERSUASION
G.H. JAMIESON

THE AGE OF ACCESS

INFORMATION TECHNOLOGY AND SOCIAL REVOLUTION

Posthumous papers of COLIN CHERRY

Compiled and edited by WILLIAM EDMONDSON

CROOM HELM
London • Sydney • Dover, New Hampshire

© 1985 William Edmondson
Croom Helm Ltd, Provident House, Burrell Row,
Beckenham, Kent BR3 1AT
Croom Helm Australia Pty Ltd, Suite 4, 6th Floor,
64-76 Kippax Street, Surry Hills, NSW 2010, Australia

British Library Cataloguing in Publication Data

Cherry, Colin
The age of access: information technology and social revolution: posthumous
papers of Colin Cherry.——(The Croom Helm information technology series)
1. Communication   2. Technological innovations
I. Title   II. Edmondson, William
302.2   P91

ISBN 0-7099-3458-0

Croom Helm, 51 Washington Street,
Dover, New Hampshire 03820, USA

Library of Congress Cataloging-in-Publication Data

Cherry, Colin.
The age of access.

(Croom Helm information technology series)
Includes index.
1. Computers — Social aspects. I. Edmondson,
William, 1946– . II. Title. III. Series.
QA76.9.C66C48 1985   303.4'834   85-16675
ISBN 0-7099-3458-0

Printed and bound in Great Britain by
Biddles Ltd, Guildford and King's Lynn

CONTENTS

SERIES FOREWORD

This series of books explores the way in which developments in information technology are changing our environment.

We are at the beginning of a communications revolution. Developments in computers, electronic equipment and telecommunications are bringing information technology to all aspects of work and leisure.

These developments are focusing our attention on the storage, retrieval and use of information, the way we communicate with others, with ourselves, and with the world.

I am pleased to add *The Age of Access: Information Technology and Social Revolution*, the posthumous papers of Colin Cherry, edited by William Edmondson to this series.

In 1981 as part of my researches into the growing uses of computers and as a follower of Colin Cherry's work for a number of years, I re-examined many of his writings and papers. To my surprise I learnt of an unfinished and unpublished manuscript but not where it was located. By one of those sets of coincidences that sometimes occur, when this series was in the planning stages, my literary agent Miss Frances Kelly, put me in touch with William Edmondson, who had been working on this material. We had previously met while I was a Visiting Research Fellow at Imperial College, London, but at that time had been unaware of each other's joint interest.

This hitherto unpublished material written by Cherry before his death in 1979, shows a startling insight into the coming information revolution. This book will add an important dimension to the debate on human issues concerned with information technology.

P.J. Hills,

FOREWORD

I appreciate the privilege of being invited to write a foreword to *The Age of Access*. Colin Cherry, a pioneer in the field of communications studies, died while he was still thinking hard about problems many of which he himself had identified. William Edmondson, one of his former students, has been able not only to make sense of Cherry's posthumous papers, many of which were sketchy or incomplete, but to provide indispensible commentary and analysis of his own. The result is a book which is bound to be of interest to communications scholars, whatever their academic discipline. I hope, too, that it will be more widely read, for communications issues are central to much current debate about structures, policies and values. It was Cherry himself who called the 'layman' 'that sternest of disciplinarians'.

I first met Cherry with the distinguished engineer Willis Jackson, who was a connoisseur of originality and boldness of purpose, and I was struck at once myself by the exploratory style of Cherry's thinking and by what the awarders of the Marconi Medal, which he was later to receive, called in their rubric 'a profound commitment to human betterment'. The quest for 'betterment' was a presupposition of his thinking, not something which it was necessary or useful to argue about.

Cherry was born in 1914 and left school in an age of uncertainty. His own personal way ahead was hard. He made it not conventionally through a university, but through evening classes after daytime work as a laboratory assistant. It was a sign both of his academic talent and of his determination that he graduated with first-class honours in engineering — and it was through engineering that he was to move after the Second World War into communications studies. He was soon writing carefully and critically on what he called 'socio-technical' issues before such writing became fashionable. Yet it is important to bear in mind that his *Pulse and Transients in Communications Circuits* preceded by more than twenty years his *World Communication: Threat or Promise?* Few other writers have followed this particular route.

Cherry, though a lone thinker, who was not the least interested in summarising or synthesising other people's facts and opinions, was nonetheless aware of the importance of communication to himself. 'True communication' he believed, 'is always an act of courage, of daring.' Yet, he found it necessary to communicate as fully as he could with psychologists, linguists, mathematicians and in his later years with historians and philosophers. He was fascinated by information theory and during a productive sabbatical leave in 1952 worked with Norbert Wiener at MIT, like Wiener, looking outside and inside his subject. When he was given the title of Henry Mark Pease Professor of Telecommunication at Imperial College, London, in 1958, the title of his inaugural lecture was 'Telecommunication as a Social Science'. 'Technology, *per se*', he insisted, 'has no power.' He did not try to predict. 'I can only speak of the present and express hope for the future', he once wrote. He used his Marconi Award to draw others into communication with each other as well as with himself.

Because of his aims and his methods some of his fragments are particularly interesting. Sometimes they are collected evidence, sometimes signposts. It is certain that had he lived he would have revised some of the things he had written. He was always ready to do a new draft. Those of us who got to know him and to appreciate the difficulties under which he laboured will be grateful for what was finished but sad that he could not finish this book himself.

Asa Briggs
Worcester College
Oxford

ACKNOWLEDGEMENTS

I am indebted to The Leverhulme Trust for their support and encouragement for my work on this book.

I am very grateful for the encouragement and assistance which I have received from Heather Cherry, Mrs Marconi Braga and the Aspen Institute for Humanistic Studies. Jeremy Barr, Harlan Cleveland and Arthur Norberg provided many invaluable comments and not a little of their time. Time and comments were also generously supplied by other members of the workshop held in December 1982 at Spring Hill Conference Center, Wayzata, Minnesota: Anne Wells Branscomb, Donald Geesaman, Nicholas Johnson, Mary Gardiner Jones, Magda Cordell McHale, Michael Rice, Walter Orr Roberts, John Rollwagen, Gerald Sophar, Charles Zracket. All participants are indebted to Lyn Krieger, of the Spring Hill Center, for her helpfulness and generosity. Ronald Stamper, although unable to attend the workshop through ill-health, contributed some materials for the discussions.

I am eternally grateful to Linda for her unstinting support and the supply of countless cups of tea and coffee.

W. Edmondson

PART ONE

MATERIALS COMPLETED BY COLIN CHERRY FOR HIS BOOK

'A Second Industrial Revolution?'

INTRODUCTION

In 1978 Professor Colin Cherry was awarded the Marconi Fellow-ship — 'To honour notable contributions to the field of communications, both in the scientific/technological sense and in terms of human perception'. The fellowship is awarded each year and the recipients are expected to undertake some specific programme of work of their own choosing.

Colin Cherry chose to do two things with his Fellowship. He used a significant portion of the award to sponsor a conference on 'The Foundations of Broadcasting Policy'. This was held in May 1980 at Leeds Castle, in south-east England.[1] He chose as his programme of work the writing of a book and he provisionally titled this 'A Second Industrial Revolution?'. When he died on 23 November 1979, Colin Cherry had completed only three chapters of the book. In addition to these chapters he left a large quantity of material which he had gathered together for use when writing the other chapters.

This book contains the completed chapters, with the original preface, together with material selected from the files for the unfinished chapters. My purpose in this introduction is threefold: to explain why it has taken five years to bring Colin Cherry's material before the public; to give a description of the material itself and how the book came to have its present form; to offer the reader some indication of why the book is important and to highlight various facets of its complex theme which seem particularly relevant to our exploration of the future. These points are taken in turn.

Towards the end of the first year following Colin Cherry's death I was asked, as one of his former students and research assistants, whether I could take on the not inconsiderable task of producing something publishable from the materials he left. My own research on communication and the deaf at that time was funded by The Leverhulme Trust and they very generously agreed to grant me time and funds for the work, to be undertaken part-time and alongside my own research.

Within a few months the three chapters which Cherry had com-pleted were in final form, with footnotes and references in order.

The plan at that stage was to organise a workshop or conference (to be held late in 1981 or early in 1982) on Cherry's writings, with the aim of eliciting some commentary essays from the participants, to accompany the finished chapters in the published volume. Despite considerable effort and enthusiasm on the part of Michael Rice and Walter Orr Roberts of the Aspen Institute for Humanistic Studies (then the administrators of the Marconi Fellowship) and Harlan Cleveland of the Hubert H. Humphrey Institute of Public Affairs, University of Minnesota (Cleveland and Cherry had met at the Aspen Institute in Colorado in the summer of 1979), the funds for such a meeting could not be secured and the plan had to be abandoned.

During the winter of 1981/2 I worked on the materials for the chapters which Cherry never tackled. The nature of the task is described in the separate introduction to the 'Notes and Fragments', the collection of notes and fragments from Cherry's files which follows the chapters. The autumn of 1982 I spent at the Hubert H. Humphrey Institute of Public Affairs, and in the December of that year the materials published here were the focus of a small informal workshop held at Spring Hill Conference Center, just outside Minneapolis. This event, made possible by the generosity of the Center, produced much interesting discussion and another plan for the book. It was decided that the 'Notes and Fragments' should be included in the final volume as they stood, without extensive explanatory or linking passages. It was considered that they were provocative and lively reading, and that they afforded an insight into Cherry's preoccupations and concerns. It was also decided that I would compose a commentary essay to accompany the assembled materials. The essay would be inspired by my own reading of the materials as well as the discussions at Spring Hill.

On this basis negotiations were held with a publisher and by the summer of 1983 the 'final' manuscript was being reviewed. The essay was in first draft form, but the shape of the book seemed about right. Included, as an appendix, were the articles which originally appeared in a *New York Times* supplement, on 23 May 1965, called 'The Information Revolution'. The intention was that these would provide illustrations of the various ways in which futuristic predictions were (and still are) made, and that as a whole they would counterpoint and illuminate Cherry's more analytical endeavours.

Following a succession of reviews, comments and rejections by several publishers, it became clear that there was a serious problem with the manuscript. The form lacked coherence and the content varied in quality and relevance. The commentary essay, although revised, was uneven but promising. The appendix was not well integrated thematically and the book lacked a focus. Cherry's own materials were not immune to criticism either. Some readers found them exciting and provocative, others considered them pedestrian or out of date. The varied response to the content was encouraging because it suggested that the topics and arguments were neither ahead of their time nor old-fashioned. The basic problem seemed to be one of format.

At this point a chance meeting with Dr Philip Hills, the editor of the Information Technology series within which this book is published, led to the suggestion of an alternative plan for the book and it is in this form that the book was finally accepted for publication. The commentary essay and the material from the *New York Times*, it was suggested, should be omitted. This book is, therefore, entirely Colin Cherry's material, although it is obviously not the finished book as he would have completed it.

The materials in the book fall into two categories: the preface and three completed chapters, and the 'Notes and Fragments'. The chapters which Cherry finished do not represent three-eighths of a larger book (the plan was for eight chapters) as they would do if the other five chapters had been completed but subsequently lost or destroyed. Furthermore, there are two separate senses in which what we have is not simply the completed portion of a larger grand plan. Cherry did indeed have a book plan, but his style of writing was definitely evolutionary. The book plan itself evolved. Three versions of what Cherry called the 'summary of the chapter contents of the book' were found. The difference between the last and the existing text for chapters 1, 2 and 3 illustrates well the organic way in which the book was taking shape as Cherry worked. As he progressed from chapter to chapter it seems that he simply wrote it out, in long-hand, revised it (extensively in the case of Chapter 3), and then moved on. At any stage in this process the form of chapters to come was apparently treated as flexible. Material originally destined for a later chapter might be utilised as desired or, alternatively, material written for the chapter in hand could be discarded and perhaps marked for later use. Likewise, notes moved back and forth through the files as the chapters took shape.

The second sense in which it can be said that Colin Cherry was not just filling in the details of something thoroughly sketched out in advance comes from the circumstances in which the third chapter was written. During the autumn of 1979, with failing health and in increasing pain, whether at home, in hospital or later, in a hospice, he laboured on this chapter, and he completed it some weeks before his death. What is significant here is not the quality of the product of this incredible determination, but its form. It would appear that as his health declined Colin Cherry brought material forward for inclusion in the chapters on which he was working (and especially Chapter 3), both in terms of the topics covered and the emphasis or space given to them.

The finished chapters are, it seems, best read as a trio of essays on the general theme of human communication, information technology and social revolution, rather than as part of something larger. However, the original intention to write a book of eight chapters shows through, and so it remains pertinent to enquire into the nature of that original intention, in so far as we can find the evidence. The 'Notes and Fragments' are published here, and in the format chosen, for this reason.

An account of the compilation of the 'Notes and Fragments' accompanies them as a specific introduction. Suffice it to say here that they provide the sort of contextual information the reader needs for a sensitive appreciation of the completed chapters. It would have been unwise, if not impossible, to have attempted to finish the book because this would have distorted the context within which Cherry was placing what he wrote. The 'Notes and Fragments', therefore, are presented with a minimum of editorial reworking or interpretation. They are presented in an order which, it is hoped, minimises the sense of thoughts scattered whilst at the same time revealing the liveliness of the mind behind the thoughts.

The importance of Colin Cherry's approach to his chosen topic is revealed as much in the 'Notes and Fragments' as in the chapters. He wrote as an individualist, someone with a point of view to express, rather than as a reviewer or synthesiser of other people's views. It is for this reason that the reader will not find in his writing many references to the recent (i.e. 1970s before 1979) published material on the topic. The significance of this is not that Cherry did not bother to read these materials or that he thought little of them (we simply do not know) but is instead that he felt able to make his point by reference to other, usually somewhat earlier, work in sociology, history of science and technology, and the like.

As part of his style Colin Cherry exhibited a keen historical sense. It was not that he wanted to write history books (he tells us explicitly that his book is not a history book), nor simply that history might have predictive value and thus be useful in answering his question. Rather, he saw very clearly the relevance both of early work in sociology and of previous events in the history of information technology, to our efforts at understanding the present. It has to be recognised that Cherry was not one of the many who like to offer their opinions of the significance of information technology on the basis of where they think it is 'taking' or 'leading' society. As Cherry stresses, the technology doesn't do these things to society. His appraisal of information technology is concerned with its current social context and the prior development of this. We can only hope to appreciate the liberties of action afforded by a radical technology such as the computer (and thus, in some sense, to look into the future) when we have a firm understanding of the circumstances of its emergence. It seems clear to me that both the socio-political context and the historical view of the evolution of the *status quo* should be of equal concern to us if we are to make sense of a question such as 'A Second Industrial Revolution?'.

The historical aspect of Colin Cherry's approach explains his denial of the applicability of the term 'revolutionary' to any technology, as well as his occasionally rather dated style and his pedantic concern that the reader understand exactly what is meant by terms like 'revolution', 'property' or 'sharing'. It is perhaps unfortunate that these terms almost instantly evoke a certain cluster of connotations with a strong contemporary bias. Whilst it is true that Cherry did not support the British Conservative Party it is equally true that his exposition is not a political tract. The sensitive reader will find this caution, and Cherry's repetitiveness in his effort to get his point across, rather irksome. However, there are certainly some other readers to whom his pedantry is appropriately directed. Cherry made no apology in this regard and I have not thought fit either to add one or to edit the chapters he completed.

Those who are familiar with Colin Cherry's previous work will recognise some of the arguments from, for example, Chapters 1 and 8 of *On Human Communication* (the manuscript for Chapter 8, added for the third edition published in 1978, was in the files for the new book). Also significant is Cherry's revision for the 1978 edition of *World Communication: Threat or Promise?* (the manuscript version of Chapter 5, section 2, was also in the files) and his work on the social significance of the telephone (see note 46, Chapter 1, for the reference). It seems clear that in the few years before his death Colin Cherry was developing some of his ideas afresh. To me it seems also clear that this development was never completed.

The main reason why I considered the book unfinishable is, therefore, simply that it would appear that Cherry had not completed his thoughts about all the issues he had raised. Why then publish the material at all? I think that there are several good and independently valid reasons for considering the unfinished book an important contribution to the debate on information technology. As already noted, one significant factor is his sensitivity to history and his concern to relate technology to social context. Other points to note are his caution in adopting fashionable terms like 'information revolution' or 'revolutionary technology', his lucid style, and the provocative nature of his arguments.

There is one reason, however, which is difficult to appreciate without a brief interpretative comment on Cherry's 'book'. I suggest that this is also useful in that it provides a guide, not only to what he wrote, but for all those who seek to engage in the debate. I submit that in essence Cherry posed himself a series of questions concerning the possible locus of the putative social revolution consequent upon the widespread adoption of information technology. The third chapter, in my view, can be considered to be addressed to a question such as 'Do we face a social revolution because of the spread of electronic brain power in society?' (in the sense that the first industrial revolution could be thought of as a consequence of the spread of mechanical muscle power). The clear answer we get is in the negative. It is conceivable that the other chapters would have considered different putative loci. However, the point of interest would appear to be the implication that by implicitly posing such questions another of Cherry's questions is revealed as yielding a positive but inadequate answer.

The first and second chapters raise, and answer affirmatively, a question concerned with social organisation. If information technology, for example the computer, is radical in Cherry's sense, and if it is correct to view this as the technology of organisation, then clearly society is faced with new liberties of action and we have 'found' our revolution. The sense of revolution in society is, therefore, caused by appreciation of new organisational possibilities, rather than by recognition that one or another new organisational pattern has emerged with its liberties of action. However, for whatever reason, Cherry seemed dissatisfied with this possibility (perhaps because it smacks of the revolution to end all revolutions, being a revolution in the potential for revolution itself).

My own view is that Colin Cherry was right to go beyond the glib answer. Furthermore, I consider that we *can* locate the sense of revolution, although I cannot say whether Cherry would have agreed with me (I think it likely). Information technology is a radical technology which affords us liberties of *mental* action. This, I consider, is why it is so important. We can view the first industrial revolution as the exploitation and exploration of liberties of physical action. The second industrial revolution, if we accept Cherry's title, goes beyond industry to society in general. It is not possible to expand this thesis here, as was attempted originally in the commentary essay, except to make one point.

The title of the book offered by Colin Cherry was always provisional. The title under which it appears here was selected because it focuses attention on the liberties of mental action afforded by the technology. These liberties all relate to the notion of access, in the colloquial sense: information access. It is the idea of access — instant, far reaching, probing, invasive, or what have you — which excites us when we think of information networks, communication systems, shopping by computer, or the educational implications of computers. Equally, it is access which frightens us when we think of data-banks, Orwell's Big Brother, or computer crime. Like Cherry I consider the word 'revolution' somewhat overworked. For me 'The Age of Access' is the most appropriate aphorism as a title for our communication fixated, interactive, interconnected future. As the full title implies, it is planned that in subsequent volumes consideration will be given to other topics within the general area set out by this book. For example, my commentary essay will be worked up into a 'reply' to Cherry's rather 'society'-dominated views. My view is that in fact the 'Age of Access', based on liberties of mental action afforded individuals, derives its most potent sense of revolution from the perspective of the individual.

The work Cherry completed and the 'Notes and Fragments' harvested from the files, amount to an important contribution to the information technology debate because we are obliged to consider our present and our past, rather than to fantasise about the future, and also because we are shown how this can be done. The fact that

Colin Cherry did not complete the book increases the value of the work. Presented with this fascinating material the reader may react as I have done, with feelings of regret that he did not live long enough to write more of what he thought on the many topics over which his interest ranged. But there is a strong emanation, from the notes as well as the completed chapters, of ideas in development, of the very discursiveness which he denied: 'With books too. We do not 'communicate' with the author *discursively*, especially if he is dead'.

To my mind Colin Cherry's writing goes quite contrary to his belief, expressed in Chapter 2, section 7, that books are part of the unilateral services. After reading the completed chapters and the notes one is left with the sense of a question — 'Well, what is *your* view?'.

Note

1. The proceedings were published as *The Future of Broadcasting*, R. Hoggart and J. Morgan (eds), Macmillan, 1982.

ACKNOWLEDGEMENT

In 1978 I was honoured by the award of the Fourth Marconi International Fellowship, which has made the writing of this book possible. I should like here to express my gratitude to the Marconi Council and to its Chairman, Mrs Marconi Braga.

Colin Cherry

PREFACE

This book is based upon lectures which I have been delivering to post-graduate students at Imperial College, London, for several years under the title 'What is Communication?' Soon after starting it became clear that it would be necessary in addition to examine another question, namely: 'What is Technology?', in a similar philosophical and sociological way. The purpose of these lectures has been to help the student to argue his way through the clamour of reports and predictions and the frequent extravagant claims made for modern 'information technology' (meaning, in the main, telecommunication and computing), and to examine what truth there may be in the idea that many today are calling the 'Second Industrial Revolution', which, they say, is now upon us. It must be emphasised that neither in these lectures nor in this book, are we concerned with futurology; no attempts at prediction are made concerning either future technological gadgets or the likely social changes that the future may hold. We confine our attention wholly to principles of argument and to examination of concepts, and leave the reader to deal with the future himself. This book is addressed to that sternest of disciplinarians, the 'layman', and no technical knowledge on his part is called for, because the main problems and points of interest are not technical in nature. Indeed, we may assume that at the technological level anything is possible today and in the future; if you can say clearly what it is you want, then there is little doubt that it can be made. The real problems lie elsewhere.

What exactly is this 'Second Industrial Revolution' which we hear so much about today? For that matter, what was the 'First'? It is noteworthy that the people who lived in the late eighteenth and early nineteenth centuries did not speak of the growth of industry and the factory system as being 'revolutionary' for they did not see it as such. The revolution that dominated that period of history was, of course, the French Revolution. Those of us today who speak of 'the Second Industrial Revolution' see it as a social movement of enormous scale, stemming from the 'explosive' developments in the electronics industry in the post-war industrial world; it is said to be based upon the 'technology of information', whereas the first (so-called) Industrial Revolution was based upon the 'technology of power'. There is a certain truth in this, but it is not enough alone to justify the use of the word 'revolution', First or Second. Certainly, to the general public some of the reports in the press can often be very alarming, as when the sheer growth in size of the multinational corporations is referred to, as dependent upon modern telecommunication systems and computers; or when the imagination is stirred by the apparent powers of computers to record our personal data and to penetrate our private lives; or when these reports tell us that our children are far more influenced by television than they are by their schooling, and that rising crime statistics are correlated with violence in television programmes.

There is nothing new in this; all radically new inventions have given rise to public concern from the moment of their inception — and for very good reason — but none more so than those which affect our powers of communicating, one with another. Anything which touches upon our knowledge or private information is seen as particularly threatening (e.g. espionage (theft of information) is a far more serious crime than shoplifting (theft of property), just as blackmail is more serious than burglary). Knowledge, it would seem, is more important than property. Certainly, the 'technology of information', of which we are speaking, may be a technology of particular importance, but we need to enquire further before judging whether it supports truly revolutionary movements. So is there anything new about the 'technology of information' that sets it quite apart from all other previous fields? I shall argue in this book that there is, for certain fundamental reasons which have nothing to do with the technology *qua* technology; the reasons lie in the nature of human communication itself which, it will be argued here, is not an 'exchange process' but is always a 'sharing process'.

This distinction is of vital importance. Most simply it can be expressed this way: if I 'send' you a message (e.g. the words on this page) I do not lose it myself, but retain it in memory or in duplicate copy. We have then *shared* it. Consequently, it is true to say that messages, unlike commodities, are not required to be lost to the 'sender' when he communicates them to another. Indeed, the word 'sender' is a misnomer; strictly, he cannot 'send' messages as he can send goods or commodities, but must always share them. On the other hand, the economic principle of 'exchange' requires the goods or commodities to be lost to the owner when they are bartered or sold for money.

The two principles are fundamentally distinct — those of

'exchange' (barter, trade) and of 'sharing' (communication). Messages do not have the nature of commodities and cannot be property. As we shall argue in Chapter 1, messages can be bought, but they literally *cannot* be sold (in the economic sense of exchange). Unlike commodities, messages may be said to have no economic rarity value, for they can be reproduced indefinitely, without loss; they are therefore not to be regarded as a finite resource (as say, oil, or paper pulp or any other physical commodities are). They are abstract, not physical. However, all these points are points of principle.

What happens in practice? The law steps in, aiming to convert messages (sources of information, knowledge) into finite resources by *legitimising* their spread to a finite group of people — as by law of copyright, of secrecy, of censorship, etc. Such attempts may be regarded by some people as ways of creating 'intellectual property' which, in principle, is something that they cannot naturally be. The ownership and transfer of goods and commodities may be regulated by law because selling them (or even giving them away) necessarily requires them to be lost to the seller (or donor), so that their possession may be checked, at any time. On the contrary, it is not possible to identify with certainty all those heads in which a particular item of knowledge may be — whether illicitly or not. Cheating, or the 'theft of knowledge', is less overt than is the theft of material goods!

Modern technology makes this abundantly clear. For example, duplicating machines have today outdated the law of copyright; again, personal information may now be filed in centralised computers, by the police, government departments, and commercial houses without the people knowing, thereby rendering them somewhat unprotected by the law.

All such argument rests on the fundamental fact that communication is a process of sharing (Latin: *communicare* = to share). However, we must be careful to note that the word *sharing* is ambiguous, having two meanings; (a) sharing by division (sharing *between*) and (b) sharing by participation (sharing *with*). Communication is sharing in this latter sense only — as when we share a common interest with someone or common membership of a club, or a common concern. Communication is, essentially, a social process. Indeed, the view to adopt here is that it is our primary social process; in Chapter 4 I shall be defining a 'social group' as *people in communication*.

With this view, one is led to the conclusion that, as an activity, communication is unique among all our activities so that, correspondingly, the technology of communication (or, if you wish, the technological extension of our powers to communicate knowledge and information) is also unique among all our various technologies: hence, we may reasonably expect its social outcomes to be radically different in nature from those of other technologies. But, we shall be asking, in what specific ways? Technology itself, in the metal, has no power whatever; the power lies in the hands of those who possess and use it. We shall here go along with the pioneer sociologist Emile Durkheim, and regard the technology possessed by any society as a *social* fact and place it alongside the law, the educational system, and other social institutions of that society, all of which are interrelated and bear upon the actions, thinking and feelings of its people. If we consider the technology of communication in particular, its uniqueness may perhaps partly be expressed by saying that it bears upon the thinking and feelings of the people in the first place (their education, attitudes, culture) most often, leading to changes in their social activities as a consequence. On the other hand, the other technologies are more likely to bear upon people's activities (what they do, their habits, etc.), leading to changes in their thinking and feelings, about themselves and about others as a consequence.

Where, now, does all this get us, with regard to our original question — i.e. what credence can we attach to the idea of the 'Second Industrial Revolution'?

Revolutions are social cataclysms, vast changes in people's values, emotions and sentiments. It will be argued here that technology alone cannot make a revolution, however radically new the inventions may be. Nevertheless, to take Durkheim's viewpoint, it may be said to be one major contributory factor, if spoken of as an *activity*, and as a social fact, rather than in terms of things, gadgets, artefacts in the metal. Thus, the (so-called) Industrial Revolution has in hindsight become seen as the rapid evolution of the social process of industrialisation, which meant far more than the great spurt in inventiveness; it was a total change in the 'way of life', in the values, emotions and sentiments of the people of certain countries. The 'triumph' of industrialisation (if you regard it as such) has been a triumph of organisation, not of technology alone.

It is the creation of the host of necessary new social institutions (governmental, financial, educational) that is the hallmark of industrialisation, not the introduction of the technology itself.

Again, this is one of the great stumbling-blocks to development in the Third World — organisation. It is no use pouring in millions of dollars' worth of machinery if the social institutions do not exist, or are not created, which are of a kind that, starting from the people's own cultural base, can adapt to the changed circumstances created by the technology.

Was this the case with those wealthy countries which industrialised early, in the eighteenth and nineteenth centuries? Did the necessary social institutions exist? Certainly, one could point out the organisation of the great estates and to various financial institutions. But these alone would not explain why the people *wanted* to change their ways of life, and desire all those changes which later came to be seen as 'industrialisation'. After all, change is uncomfortable. So what drove them to it? What was peculiar about the values, emotions and sentiments of the people of that time that started them on the path which has led to our present day world of industry and business — not only this, but also made them *desire* to do so?

It was Max Weber who pointed out that those countries which first developed capitalist industry were countries of Puritan background (where the word 'capitalist', to Weber, merely referred to the accumulation of capital for investment — whether coming from private sources or, as in the USSR, from state sources). More particularly, he observed that the system of beliefs of the later Calvinists more or less compelled them to set out on this path of industrial 'progress'. We shall be taking a look at some of Weber's arguments which, although known to be controversial, seem relevant to many of today's problems — not only within the industrial countries but also those of the Third World having various philosophic/religious backgrounds. We shall be paying special attention to the 'technology of information' (telecommunications and computers, in particular). Whether or not this technology, which is expanding at a truly explosive rate today, justifies our speaking of a 'Second Industrial Revolution', there is no doubt whatever that it is of increasing importance both to the development of the Third World and to its relationships with the industrialised countries, whilst it is causing mounting concern to them at the same time.

Colin Cherry
Imperial College
University of London

A Second Industrial Revolution?

Colin Cherry

1   A SECOND INDUSTRIAL REVOLUTION?

The world will never starve for want of wonders; but only for want of wonder. (G.K. Chesterton), *Tremendous Trifles.*

1. Our Love/Hate Relationship with Technology

The cornucopia of technology continues to pour out its abundance of artefacts; labour-saving devices, gadgets, instruments, tools, machines and machines to make machines — with which the public has adopted a kind of love/hate relationship, at least within the industrialised countries. On the one hand, people never seem satisfied, but want more of them; they love their automobiles, their television sets, their self-cleaning, encapsulated, multi-purpose, fully programmed automated what-nots. Yet at the same time technology itself is the target of much criticism; it is blameworthy and some people are frightened that 'one day it may take over the world'. Science fiction is packed with robots and technological horrors. Why should these dual emotions arise?

The first and simplest answer may be offered to the man-in-the-street, the domestic user, the inexpert (which means all of us at various times). It is that, whereas in the earlier centuries people made their own tools and utensils and developed skills for using them, this is no longer true today, not only in the industrialised countries but also in the Third World wherever modern technology has gone (e.g. transistor radio sets in Indian villages). In the social anthropologists's terms, the producers and consumers were once the same people, but they are no longer.[1] People are now surrounded by artefacts which they did not make themselves and could not possibly do so. Few of the millions of people who have a television set know how it works, let alone how to make one, nor are they interested, for they can use them without such knowledge and with no skill whatsoever. Neither do many understand the operation of telephone exchanges, nor of micro-processors, nor of aircraft, nor even of simple slot-machines. Nor do they need to, for that can be left to that ever-more dominant figure — 'the expert'. We are in his hands. The Do-It-Yourself movement today flourishes not only for economic reasons, but also because there is an elementary satisfaction in making and doing, if only simple things — above all when it frees us a little from the stranglehold of 'the expert'. But we know that we rely upon him utterly for the satisfactory working of modern technology. We love our domestic machinery so long as it works well; and when it breaks down we love the maintenance engineer even more — though it is the love of a slave for his master.

Almost anyone can take their television set to pieces, or their automobile, or even a computer, and reduce them to their elemental parts, laid out on the floor, if they feel so inclined. But they could not necessarily put them together again, because they would lack that abstract thing — the necessary information, the knowledge about how the parts are to be related.

The word *know* is ambiguous and can be used in several distinct senses. We say that we know how to operate a television set, but we may not know how it operates. In earlier times people would not have felt such a sharp distinction between these two forms of knowing; they would know how to use a bow-and-arrow, and accepted this knowing how it worked because they made them. Our sharp distinctions today have been largely the result of another kind of knowledge — scientific knowing. Scientific knowing is an objective matter implying that a specification, (theory, model) can be made that is independent of the user and is universal; it is 'knowledge without a knower'.[2] The bow and arrow works, not 'because I pull the string back and my bow bends, and I made it like that' etc., but because of forces, tensions, bending-moments and other abstractions.

Our love/hate relation with technology appears in another form which touches less the man-in-the-street (the domestic user) but concerns more the one I shall term 'the philosopher', meaning anyone who is thoughtful about our long-term future, about likely effects of our rapidly expanding computer and communication systems (called here, for convenience, 'information technology') upon future patterns of employment (or unemployment?), or about whether such changes can conceivably give real meaning to the expression 'the age of leisure', or anyone who is concerned with the likely consequences of the growing economic gap between the industrial and the Third World countries, or whether the cornucopia of technology is really bottomless or, if not, whether and how our human resources and policies may come to restrict its flow — that is to say, anyone concerned seriously with all these problems which the 'technology of information' appears to raise and which occupy increasing space in our newspapers. Indeed, we shall argue in this book that the 'technology of information' *must* raise such questions and problems, for they are inherent in its nature; it is a very special technology, unique in the history of industrialisation. In order to present such argument it will be necessary to examine two particular questions — both of which may be given glib and popular answers, but which actually are more difficult to answer than they may seem. These questions are:

(1) What is communication?
(2) What is technology?

The first question is commonly answered by saying 'communication is sending messages'; we shall here contradict this, for it is nothing of the kind. The second question is usually answered by saying that 'technology is man-made things, artefacts'; however, this answer is inadequate. Others have clarified the question by distinguishing various classes of technology[3] — e.g. toys, tools, instruments, machines, 'cybernetic' machines, etc., but we shall not be concerned with making such distinctions for the purpose of this book[4], although they are valid distinctions. We shall be speaking of technology in general and of 'information technology' in particular, with the aim of clarifying the many questions about both communication and technology which so frequently concern the general public and 'the philosopher' today. It seems to me that both subjects are widely misunderstood, and that it is not always for the right reasons that either modern technology or communication are so often criticised. Both subjects attract a great deal of popular wisdom today, a deal of false argument and frequently fears about the sort of future into which this 'information technology' may be leading us. We shall be concerned particularly with this flowering of electronics which will be called, for convenience, 'information technology', symbolised by such things as computers, satellites of many kinds, television, global telephoning, micro-processors (the 'chip'), and whatever other devices that the future may hold which affect our powers of assembling and communicating information. However, no technical knowledge of electronics will be required of the reader. Is there something special about this modern 'information technology' that distinguishes it from earlier technologies which causes it to raise major new problems?

We shall be arguing here that there is, and that this difference is the source of the love/hate relation which even the one whom I have termed 'the philosopher' shows. The difference is such as to lead many people to speak about a 'Second Industrial Revolution'. What justification can there be for such a phrase? The answer most commonly given is that, whereas the (so called) Industrial Revolution, stemming from the mid-eighteenth century, was based upon the technologies of power and production, the Second Revolution will be based upon the technology of information. But a simple statement of this kind gives neither justification for use of the phrase, nor does it offer any explanation as to why the social consequences of 'information technology' are likely to be truly 'revolutionary', nor does it give us any guidance as to the nature of the likely consequences. We shall need to examine far more deeply into what is so special about 'information technology'.

Understanding of the workings of modern electronic equipment requires ever increasing scientific knowledge, although to operate it usually does not. Design of such equipment too has become increasingly a scientific matter; but the ultimate product is technological, and it will be judged and valued technologically (its reliability, convenience etc.), not scientifically. This is true not merely of the domestic user with his television set or his pocket calculator, but equally of the professional; his usage of the most elaborate equipment need make no *scientific* demands upon him, whilst its design increasingly makes such demands upon its designer. The gulf between the designer and the user has today opened into a chasm whilst unfortunately it has also led to popular confusion between science and technology as human activities. The two distinct historical processes, science and technology, differ in their histories, their social values, their responsibilities, their methods and their goals. The point is being pressed here because this distinction is vital to the arguments being presented in this book. It is essentially technology with which we shall be concerned and not with the scientific principles underlying its design.

In spite of the fact that modern electronic 'technology of information' increasingly requires science for its design, it is equally true to say that an 'over-scientific' attitude to technology may sometimes be inhibiting, by which I mean no more than it may inhibit courage to act before scientific theory exists or is fully understood. Science is an unending quest, whilst the creation of any technological product requires decision and action — which consequently must always be carried out in partial scientific ignorance. This is an inevitable fact, not to be despised; it is inherent in the nature of technology.

There is probably no better example of such an inhibitory 'over-scientific' danger than that shown by the invention of radio itself, three-quarters of a century ago. Guglielmo Marconi,[5] who was not academically trained as a scientist, but who was rather an amateur with enormous insight, courage and enthusiasm, as well as being a business man, pursued his experiments with radio to ultimate practical success, *in spite of* warnings by Heinrich Hertz, one of the greatest scientists of the day. Hertz argued that it would require 'a mirror as large as the Continent' and would be impracticable.[6] Marconi realised one most important point, namely, that if a technological experiment should fail, it may not matter very much; but if it succeeds the consequences can be of overwhelming importance. Marconi also appreciated another difference between technology and science:

> Long experience has, however, taught me not always to believe in the limitations indicated by purely theoretical considerations. These — as we well know — are based on insufficient knowledge of all the relevant factors.[7]

These words were written by Marconi a long time ago, but they are still true today. In spite of the great increase in the usuage of science in technological design, no technological venture can rest wholly upon scientific criteria.

Technology today is virtually inseparable from the great institutions of industry, and although science may be widely and increasingly used in the design of an industry's products the choice of what those products should be is not primarily a scientific matter, but is rather one of company *policy*. These policies depend upon available capital, manpower, plant, market predictions, the insight and wisdom of its directors, etc.; they may ultimately be decided upon by people remote from science. It is in this sense that the view will be adopted, throughout this book, that technology is essentially a political matter. The goals of industry are pragmatic, not idealistic. Industrial production is always constrained by capital, law and time; it cannot wait or the firm may go bankrupt. It requires numerous empirical decisions to be made which cannot always wait for theory. It is responsible to the law (e.g. public or employees' protection). Its products which are advertised and sold may certainly be regarded as 'hypotheses' which are experimentally tested in the market, but in contrast to scientific method the hope is always that such hypotheses are correct,[8] for there is no value whatever in commercial failure! The expression 'pure science' may have a grain of sense in it, but to speak of 'pure technology' is pure nonsense. Technology is a socio-political matter and is meaningless outside a specific social context, as will be discussed in Chapter 2.

However, I may be treading dangerous ground and it will be simpler to distinguish science and technology in other ways, in particular the anthropological way.

2. Man is 'the Tool Maker and Tool User'

Man has been described by anthropologists as 'the maker and user of tools', whilst we ought perhaps to add the words: *in unlimited variety*.[9] *All* human beings are, and always have been, technological creatures. Technology is essential to Man's nature — his making and using of artefacts in unlimited variety, from palaeolithic stone axes to modern micro-processors. The pioneer sociologist Emile Durkheim (1858-1917)[10] stressed that 'society' meant not only people, but people together with the objects which they use[11]. It is also a view that is in line with modern social anthropology, which has emphasised the importance of the technologies of communication and transport, in particular.[12] Durkheim stressed that in order that a recognisable social group should become created out of an otherwise amorphous collection of individuals, there should be forces at work which were external to each of those individuals. Such forces could be their law, their moral code, their political institutions, etc., *but essentially including their technology*.

To quote Durkheim (in translation) from, perhaps surprisingly, his famous study of suicide, originally published in 1897.[13]

First, it is not true that society is made up only of individuals; it also includes material things, which play an essential role in the common life. The social fact is sometimes so materialized as to become an element of the external world. For example, a definite type of architecture is a *social* phenomenon; but it is partially embodied in houses and buildings of all sorts which, once constructed, become autonomous realities, independent of individuals. It is the same with the avenues of communication and transportation, with instruments and machines used in industry or private life which express the state of technology at any moment in history, of written language, etc. Avenues of communication which have been constructed before our time give a definite direction to our activities, depending on whether they connect us with one or another country.

Durkheim is here placing the technology of any society alongside its law, its political institutions, systems of education, etc. equally as a *social* fact, created by and perpetuated by the society, whilst emphasising that such social facts react back upon the individual and help make him a member of that society.[14] The physical environment in which people live is not wild nature, but one that has been licked into shape with the tools, the technologies, which those people possess. It is largely 'man-made'. The fields and highways, the towns and cities, railways and airways of industrial societies are social facts, as are the baked mud or wooden huts of the most primitive agricultural community. And, in Durkheim's terms, these 'give definite direction' to the people's activities.[15]

This recognition of technology as being a social fact, alongside law, religion, education and other social facts is revealed by the ways by which we often refer to different historical periods or different societies by name. Thus, we sometimes use social, cultural or political terms, as when we speak of the 'pre-Christian era', or of 'medieval times', or of 'feudalism', etc., but we often use purely technological distinctions and speak of 'the Bronze Age', 'neolithic times', 'the Age of Steam', 'The Space Age'. This way of regarding technology, which emphasises its social nature and social function, takes attention away from the popular view of it as material things, artefacts, gadgets, and highlights its essentially *active* nature. Technology is not comprehensible, it has no meaning if regarded simply as things — but viewed in terms of social activity, it is and does. It is an activity natural to all human beings, 'the tool makers and tool users', and has been from the dawn of history,[16] though of very various degrees and kinds. By contrast science, as an analytical discipline is not, but is understood only by a relatively small part of the human race and has been for a relatively short period of man's history. Man has continually sought to improve his tools by trial and error and luck. Already by the time of early Egypt people were using the wheel, sailing ships, looms, and tackle for lifting and hauling. True, the early Egyptians also saw the dawn of science, but to what small priesthood was that activity confined — knowledge that was 'ascribed to the revelation of the gods'?[17]

Throughout man's history his particular technology has not only 'given definite direction' to his practical powers of action but, equally important, has consequently had profound effects upon both his thinking and his feelings — his attitudes towards his environment, towards himself, and towards others.[18] Of course, such a statement does not mean that the particular technology possessed by some community at some particular time in history will itself decide how those people will act, think, and feel (which would imply 'historical determinism'). For there are a lot of other external forces at work upon them, such as their social customs and institutions, possible military or economic threats from outside, even the climate. Their technology merely offers them certain powers and styles of action; a new invention may radically change these powers, but what the people actually *do* with their new-found powers is not readily predictable, if only because we do not know their future conditions. Few inventions, if any, remain in use solely for the purposes for which their inventors first conceived them.

Whenever the word 'technology' is mentioned people naturally think of specific artefacts, things of the present day and familiar to them, such as television sets, automobiles, computers; but for the purpose of this book we shall adopt a more general and philosophical view of the nature of technology so as not to confine ourselves to present-day examples, but to embrace whatever the future may produce. In Chapter 2 we shall look further into this notion of technology as human activity — as 'possible modes of human actions'.

Man's drive, as a tool-maker and tool-user, leads him to create not only all forms of tools and machinery[19] and other physical artefacts but also many forms of human artefact as well — the deliberate and planned organisation of many forms of human institution. A committee, a government department, a bureau, or an administration are just as much artefacts as are machine tools. They are deliberately planned and structured; one individual may leave or resign his office, and someone else takes his place, but the machinery goes on working. Do we not speak about the 'machinery of government', or of 'handling people' just as we speak of handling tools? Our abilities to plan and create new forms of social organisation exhibit our creative 'technological' powers just as do our abilities to invent new artefacts, new technology; both are necessary and are of equal importance for industrial development. The introduction of new artefacts and techniques into the industrial scene calls for corresponding adjustments to the administrative 'machinery' if any benefit is to accrue, especially if these innovations are truly radical. This seems to be an inevitable price to be paid for industrial 'progress'. New technology calls for appropriate changes to be made in industrial organisation through which it can exert its powers; otherwise frustration results.

This is true, not only within industry itself, but generally throughout industrial society. On the whole, it would seem that we are more able and ready to create new technological artefacts than we are to devise new social organisations, new administrative 'machinery', so as to derive benefit from them. That is, we are more ready and able to adjust our material environment (our technology) to satisfy ourselves than we are to adjust ourselves (our social institutions, our customs, priorities and morals) to the environment.

Briefly, modern industrialised man finds it easier to adjust his environment to suit himself than to adjust himself to suit the environment. Man has this unique, creative, inventive, organising drive which promises him so much yet, at the same time, threatens him with destruction. It has been well said that: 'human nature is almost against nature'. It has always been so. Man is the restless creature who cannot leave things alone; wherever we look around this world we see where he has been, from the evidence of both his constructive and destructive powers, his organising and disorganising activities. We see 'the man-made world' as being distinct from 'the natural world', a distinction which stems not so much from their physical natures as from the fact that our *understandings* of them differ radically. We shall later be looking at this distinction through the eyes of the eighteenth-century philosopher Giambattista Vico (Chapter 3, Section 4).

Man appears to be unique in this respect within the animal kingdom. Whereas the lower creatures may change and adapt to their environment at the inordinately slow pace of evolution over many generations, man changes his ways, as well as his environment, infinitely faster, over historic times and, quite perceptibly, over one lifetime in the industrialised world. His inventiveness enables him to exist in any environment, from the bottom of the sea to outer space. It would appear that this ability distinguishes him not only in degree, but also in kind, from the rest of the animal kingdom. Man's changes do not depend upon chance, or evolutionary processes — he can *plan, imagine, organise* because he can manipulate internal symbols, icons and images in his head. He can *conceptualise* and *verbalise*; he can not only perceive things 'as they are', but may conceive something different, and express it. He not only communicates with his fellow men but, essentially, with himself — in thought or with internal musings.

Although it is true to say that the particular technologies which exist within a society will greatly influence the ways in which its people act, think and feel about themselves and others, it is not the material artefacts themselves which mainly distinguish that society from others. What is more significant is how the possession of the technologies is organised within the society — a political matter. For example, what particular sections of the population possess them and control their use? How are their activities controlled, if at all? How are policies for their usage decided, and by whom? How are the usages financed? There are endless such questions; the word 'possession' is so ambiguous. It is essentially the mode of possession, a political matter, which decides what *activities* are open to the people. For example, development in the Third World countries may not be helped at all (and may even be hindered) by their acquiring modern technological equipment of certain kinds *unless at the same time they can create and run the necessary organisations to make use of it, to operate and maintain it* in ways that are culturally acceptable.[20] This, of course, is not to say that they need only simple technology because they lack the technical knowledge or ability to operate any other. Far from it; they may have large numbers of trained engineers yet not be organised so as to make use of them. More than technical equipment itself, it is rather the immense problem of social organisation that provides the biggest headaches in technical aid for development in the Third World — problems of education and training, of financial control, of management, of goals, of planning, etc. — all those problems that have long faced the industrialised countries and which have led to creation of their own peculiar forms of institutions for tackling them. But there is no reason to believe that these may provide the best models for Third World countries, with their different traditions; the danger is that their desire to possess the technology, as symbolic of 'modernisation', may lead them to contempt for their own traditions. It is only too easy for ourselves, within the industrial countries, to forget the terrible social price that we too have had to pay for our industrial 'progress' and, in some ways, that we have not yet fully paid off, even today.[21]

If industrialisation be regarded as a 'triumph' (and that depends upon your values) it is essentially a triumph of organisation, very painfully won, but not a triumph attributable to the invention and introduction of material artefacts, the tools and machinery, alone. It was the creation of specialised institutions which have enabled the technology to become an *organised activity* that was the key. Early civilisations produced considerable technology, including much that is familiar within industry today (e.g. China). Hero of Alexandria invented a steam engine, but it remained no more than a toy.[22]

3. The 'Bureaucratic' Base of Modern Technology and Industry

The factor that so clearly distinguishes our modern industrial civilisation from all earlier forms is its highly organised, impersonal, and essentially rational, 'bureaucratic' nature, where the word 'bureaucracy'[23] is used not in its popular, present-day derogatory sense, but in the strict sense as used by the great social theorist, Max Weber (1864-1920). Economic life needs *structure*;[24] that structure, that organisational element, that 'bureaucracy' rests upon communication — in all its modes. Its functionaries handle 'information' (knowledge, data, words, facts and figures) rather than material commodities; their values to economic life are not so readily measured as are the various elements of the productive side of industry, and are not so readily integrated into economic theory as it stands at present.[25] One possible reason for this will be examined in Section 6.

This word 'bureaucracy' is here used in its strict sense, as stated already, to mean the many human artefacts which serve as tools for organisation. They are the machinery for producing, not goods or commodities, but something quite abstract — namely, organisation; the mechanism by which these human artefacts operate is 'communication', a concept which is not so vague and too general to admit of analysis (as so frequently is said), but one which can be clarified and opened to discussion, as we shall attempt to do so in Section 6 of this introductory chapter.

Unfortunately, this word 'bureaucracy' is so often used today in a derogatory sense; it can even alarm people, understandably. For the same love/hate relation with the public exists here as it exists with other technologies, which was referred to at the opening of this Chapter (Section 1). On the one hand, bureaucracies can be seen as servants, as machines that smooth our way through the complex modern world; on the other hand, they can be felt to be arrogant masters, privileged professionals, an elite who see their dominant position as a native right and whose function is to preserve the bureaucratic machine itself. All expertise, specialisation, or professionalism concentrates information and, therefore, power. It is so often a two-faced Janus, as seen by the general public, in our increasingly technological world; and it is this uncertainty in the mind of the man-in-the-street that is the source of his love/hate relationship with bureaucracy today.

However, we are not here concerned with making value-judgements of 'bureaucracy', but are using the word only in the morally neutral sense of Max Weber, to refer to the highly organised, rational[26] and impersonal element of modern industrial society, the human machinery which gives modern economic life its structure, structure which needs communication in order to explain its organisation and operation.

And we, the public, judge and value this bureaucratic machinery by its *efficiency*, as we would judge other machinery, although added to which we assume its *integrity*, just as we assume *reliability* in other machinery. Such integrity is not based upon kinship nor baksheesh, but upon trust in abstract offices. In industrial societies we must trust 'the manager', 'the tax collector', the 'chief accountant', 'the inspector', etc. who are not our kinsmen and whom we may never have met. That is to say, we must trust the office itself, not the particular individual holding the office at that time; he may be changed, but the office continues; the machinery goes on working. In that situation baksheesh becomes interpreted as bribery, because it *ought* to be unnecessary, just as kinship ought to be irrelevant; but this is no reason why this should make us feel morally superior in industrial societies.

It is this rational, disciplined, 'bureaucratic' element of modern industrial societies which operate with defined goals and objectives, to which Max Weber drew attention when he wrote of 'the Protestant Ethic'.[27] The individuals within it are functionaries, who do their jobs and are judged by their efficiency, their competence, jobs that are unrelated to their domestic lives; they operate by rules, and discipline is essential. Max Weber referred to this as 'the spirit of capitalism' where the term 'capitalism', as he used it, applied universally, whether the capital be provided privately, collectively, or by the state (as in the USSR). He argued that the goal of capitalism was not profit but accumulation. The ownership is irrelevant; it may change, yet the system will remain. For instance, when the British House of Commons passed the Bill to nationalise the coalmines in 1946,[28] one prominent Labour MP leapt to her feet and made the unfortunate exclamation: '*We* are the masters now!' It seemed for a moment that nothing had changed.[29]

This 'bureaucratic' organisational element is the hallmark of modern industry, rather than the machinery itself, for technology-in-the-metal has no power in itself, none whatever;[30] the power lies in the hands of those who have it and essentially in their abilities to organise social institutions for making use of it. The basis of organisation is communication. Indeed, one definition of 'communication' (and there are many others) could be given as 'the potential for organisation'. And, more than any other field of technology, it is our modern electronic information technology in particular, from telephones to micro-processors, which has developed with accelerating pace since the end of World War II, that has aroused some dramatic images in the public mind and has seriously suggested such ideas as that of a 'Second Industrial Revolution'. We shall be examining in this book whether such ideas have any genuine foundation.

4. How Realistic is the Idea of 'Post-industrial Society'?

Many writers have called attention to the great expansion — indeed, 'explosive' expansion may not be a misnomer — of this 'bureaucratic', organisational element of modern industrial society, especially commenting upon its dependence on the technologies of information (telecommunication, computing etc.). It is an expansion that has occurred since World War II, with rapid acceleration since the 1950s. There is much talk today of an 'information explosion', or of 'a knowledge explosion'. What credence can be attached to such notions?

Evidence of the trends has been given in terms of employment categories, particularly by the relative numbers of people who are employed in all forms of white-collar, organisational services (e.g. clerical, computing, financial, communication, teaching, planning, etc.) compared to those employed in actual blue-collar, productive work. It has been pointed out, by others, that soon about one half of the working populations of the highly industrial countries will be employed in one or other of the former occupations. There is other, and I think, better, evidence of the trends.[31]

These very rapid changes in the social structure of the industrial countries has led many to speak of 'the Post-industrial Society',[32] or of 'the Information Society', or even of 'a Second Industrial Revolution', expressions which writers frequently justify by saying that, whereas the so-called Industrial Revolution of the past two centuries was a revolution based upon the technologies of power (steam engines, railways, electricity, etc.) and of production, the present-day dramatic changes are more based upon knowledge and information and their technologies (especially computers and communication services, for these are tools of organisation rather than tools of production). It has been argued by others that the so-called Industrial Revolution, being based upon the technologies of power and production, led to competition for the limited material resources of the world whereas, on the contrary, the new 'technologies of information' are not constrained by limited resources (as will be explained in Section 6), so it might seem that there is hope that these newer technologies will contribute to co-operation rather than to competition. However, as we shall see later, the matter is not as simple as that.

We have referred above to the Industrial Revolution as being 'so-called' for good reason. We should not speak lightly of revolution. Revolutions are social cataclysms, sudden and immense changes in people's values, ethics, beliefs, loyalties, and sentiments. They cannot be explained by technology alone, however radical the inventions may be or however suddenly they appear on the market. To explain the Industrial Revolution as being the result of the invention of the steam engine is almost like explaining the French Revolution by the invention of the guillotine. I shall not attempt to explain either here, for this is not a history book, but there are certain points to be made that do concern our subject.

It may surprise some readers to learn that the expression 'Industrial Revolution' did not appear before the late 1870s, when it was used by Arnold Toynbee in his lectures delivered at Oxford and elsewhere. The title first appeared in print as the title of his book, published posthumously in 1884.[33] During the preceding 130 years or so, those people who had actually witnessed and even experienced the social consequences of industrialisation, with its horrors of exploitation (as they may seem to us today) and many triumphs of reform, did not speak of 'revolution', for it did not appear to them as such. They saw it rather as evolution and spoke of it as 'progress in the industrial arts' or as 'the spread of manufacture'.[34] The real revolution that shook Europe to its foundations was, of course, the French Revolution, to which the expression 'the Industrial Revolution' later became a kind of punning analogy. If we seek a truly revolutionary source for our modern industrialised, business world we must look back to the Reformation.[35]

So it would appear that the historical period so often called 'the Industrial Revolution' today was recognised as being revolutionary only in hindsight.[36] But those of us who would speak of the present-day phase of industrialisation in terms of 'post-industrial society' or of 'a Second Industrial Revolution' are not doing so in hindsight, but are doing so with all our knowledge of the social outcomes of the 'First' Industrial Revolution (as it should logically be termed). We cannot truthfully say what the future social outcomes will be, for these depend upon much more than new technology alone. But we may validly put the question another way and ask ourselves this: Are there good reasons for believing that the social effects of the new 'technologies of information' will be radically distinct from the social effects of the 'technologies of power' which we and our forefathers have already experienced? Or, put another way, are the times in which we live today, or are about to enter, so very different as to be considered as a Second Industrial Revolution — or are they merely a continuation of the 'First' Industrial Revolution?

We can say immediately that the 'First' Industrial Revolution is still continuing, because new sources of power are still being sought and with renewed vigour (atomic energy, solar energy, synthetic petroleum, etc.). But this fact does not preclude the possibility of a 'second' revolution having started; it is at least a subject worthy of discussion.

As stated before, the so-called Industrial Revolution of the past two centuries, still continuing today, has become seen as a 'revolution' based upon the technologies of power and of production whilst the present-day dramatic changes (seen by many as a Second Industrial Revolution) are based upon information and knowledge, and upon the technologies for assimilating and communicating these (the 'technologies of information'). Inasmuch as the technologies of power may be regarded as the 'tools of production', the newer technologies of information may equally well be seen as the 'tools of organisation' — tools which are essential to the creation and operation of all forms of *services* — including industrial production itself.

Whether we accept the idea of a Second Industrial Revolution, or not, it is true to say that *services* are becoming increasingly prominent today; the emphasis is shifting from employment in production to employment in all forms of service industry and from 'product markets' towards 'service markets', in the USA and other highly industrialised countries.[37] Both are utterly dependent upon the organising power offered to us by the 'technologies of information'.

But the term 'services' is ambiguous. It is also over-simple to divide a population sharply into white-collar (service) and blue-collar (production) groups. If the social trends are quoted merely in terms of the ratio of these two, the process is what is sometimes called *de-industrialisation*; in order to consider whether these trends constitute a 'Second Industrial Revolution' we must first clarify the use of the word *services*.

For our present purpose it is necessary to distinguish between two classes of services: (a) those provided by institutions directly serving the population, its welfare, interests, education, etc. (e.g. the social services, hospitals, broadcasting, schools, police, defence); and (b) the various 'information services', which render their organisation and operation possible (e.g. the telephone service, computer-links, postal service, publishing house). It is the latter which concern us for the present, the 'information services', which contribute essentially to our human powers of organisation; that is to say, they contribute to the 'bureaucratic', rational element of industrial society. However, these organising powers, now increasingly being offered us, may serve not only the amoral, economic, goals of production, but also, and equally well, may serve the social values implicit in the various services (a) above, which are more concerned with the quality of life and so cannot be amoral. It is solely this latter contribution which justifies any talk of a *Second* Industrial Revolution — even accepting that the modern trends are truly 'revolutionary' at all.

We have been arguing, so far, that certain social trends being witnessed in the more highly industrialised countries today, notably in the USA, may have been encouraged by the very rapid expansion of the 'technology of information' (mainly communication and computation), because these modern technologies are essentially tools for organisation rather than tools for production or for power. If this be a valid argument, it renders such technologies absolutely unique; but the elemental facts underlying this claim will be held over until Section 6 of this chapter.

McHale has argued that it is meaningful to speak of 'Post-industrial Society' when smaller and declining numbers of productive workers are needed to sustain industrial productivity (or even to increase it), and that this would not only mean a great change in the basis of a country's economy, but also would compel an immense change of social values (e.g. roles, statuses, assumed rights, and privileges),[38] as *services* of all kinds increasingly come to be valued as producers of real wealth, just as manufacturing industry and business are often valued as being productive of money-wealth in the present day, as ends in themselves, a 'game', the success of which is assessed by the balance sheet alone.[39]

There are several ways in which these social trends may be demonstrated. For example:

(1) *By trends in employment.* Parker, drawing upon the work of Porat,[40] has demonstrated that the statistics of employment in the USA since 1860[41] show an accelerating growth of employment in the 'information services', which by 1978 represented nearly half the working population, with a steady decrease of employment in direct industrial and agricultural production.[42]

(2) *By trends in uses of national income.* The percentage of the GNP of the United States that represents 'information services' shows similar trends.[43]

(3) *By trends in personal income disposal.* The percentage of personal income devoted to both personal information services (such as legal, financial, educational, counselling services) and to 'information technology' (such as telephones, books, magazines, television, etc.) has also been rising rapidly.[44]

The details of these remarkable trends within the highly industrialised countries need not concern us here; they are well documented. The trends are clear although some of the statistics are imprecise owing to the difficulty of defining many of the categories. However, we must be careful not to attribute these trends merely to the vast improvement in efficiency and speed of operation of modern 'information technology' itself. Revolutions are social phenomena and technology alone cannot account for them. It is true to say that, by using a modern computer of modest cost a single arithmetical or clerical operation can be done in a few millionths of a second that would take a clerk ten minutes; furthermore, the cost of doing that operation would be several million times cheaper too.[45]

But we should not be impressed by mere speed. Similarly, a telephone message travels millions of times faster than do letters in the post; however, the great social impact of the telephone service has not mainly been caused by its speed, but by something far more fundamental that will be discussed later, in Chapter 2.[46]

It is more important to regard these social trends today as part of the political process in the industrial countries. For example, not only are the numbers of people employed in 'information services' rapidly increasing, but also this employment is increasingly financed from state resources and increasingly answerable to the state. Again, the trends require corresponding changes in education, and lead to changes in class structure and in various social values. At the same time, businesses and industries are increasingly able to disperse over wide areas, even around the world, yet are regularly able to link together through telephone services and computer networks. Manufacture of complex goods, such as automobiles, need no longer be centralised; engines can be made in one country, batteries in another and bodies in yet another — but the person who buys the goods need have no notion of this. The international corporation is firmly with us; modern communication services have not merely rendered possible the large-scale, complex organisation of our industrial, business world possible, but have also rendered it *conceivable*.

This highly organised, goal-directed, rational 'bureaucratic' world of the industrialised countries today has been supported and encouraged by the explosive growth of information technology in post-war years, but it cannot be said to have been *caused* by it; for, as argued before, technology is dead-metal and has no power in itself. Why has this 'information explosion' occurred? Why should such remarkable developments have taken place within this particular field of technology and not within others? Is there something special about the 'technology of information' which distinguishes it from all others?

Many other fields of technology are advancing fast today (atomic energy, chemical engineering, aircraft) but to nothing like the same degree. So there must be something about the 'technology of information' which ensures that it encourages social outcomes which many people see and speak of, in all seriousness, as 'revolutionary'. We shall argue later, in Section 6, that indeed there is.

5. Technology Alone Does Not Make a Revolution

As said before, we should not speak too lightly of 'revolution'. Revolutions are social affairs, involving great changes in values, emotions and sentiments. Emile Durkheim spoke of society as moulding the individual, being the source of (a) his ideals, and (b) an object of his devotion, (c) belief, (d) respect and (e) adoration;[47] all may be disturbed by revolution. But also, as mentioned before, he regarded society as people together with the artefacts which they *use* (italics mine); that is, with their technology.[48]

It would therefore not seem unreasonable to assume that, when major technological changes occur in a society there will be some counter-acting adjustments to these various human values, emotions and sentiments; but it would be wrong to say that these technological changes were the sole cause, for many other forces are at work, political, economic, religious, etc. People must continually seek to adapt to technological change, in behaviour as well as in their attitudes and feelings. For example, we speak today of the 'consumer society' with feelings of guilt; we need only to remember too the changes brought about by the coming of the railways, or the immense moral and religious struggles which followed the introduction of printing into Europe or, above all, the moral, political and idealistic repercussions of the atom bomb and other military technology. It is in this existential sense that technology exerts enormous power over people, either by their possessing it or by their awareness of others possessing it. The sort of person you feel yourself to be depends very much upon the technology that you possess; if you have nothing but a stone axe you feel as one kind of person, but if you belong to society which has computers, aircraft, cars, telephones and other modern technology you feel quite different. You will feel about yourself and your rights, and about other people and *their* place in the world quite differently. But, to repeat, it would be quite wrong to regard these artefacts as the *cause*; rather they form a major contribution to how you feel in your specific social situation. For example, you place immense *trust* in your telephone, your car, your deep-freezer, your central-heating (if you have such things), and when any of these break down, or if your airways or railways are crippled by a labour strike, you will be momentarily, outraged. It *ought* not to happen to you; it is felt as a kind of moral offence.

The creation of industries and development of technology has come to be seen by so many people today as essentially 'progressive'.

This I cannot deny to anyone living in a less industrialised society than my own. However, the history of the past 200 years has shown that there are contradictions built into this concept of 'progress';[49] it always demands some social price.[50] Invention and the creation of new technologies is an irreversible process; what has been invented cannot be un-invented; it may be forgotten or fall out of use, but if it is adopted and spreads then we can say that a *want* has been created (a market) which may soon become felt as a *need*. Under conditions of rapid technological change people are under a certain stress, the stress of continually needing to readjust their thinking, feeling and behaviour. They must change their habits, or obstinately refuse to and retain their old ways; moral change must be compelled; values must be modified.[51] We need call to mind no better example than our ready acceptance of the slaughter on the roads, or of air and soil pollution by industry, or of radioactive waste from nuclear power stations; technology can only be had at some social price, and some of the prices that we have paid have been terrible. There is nothing natural or fixed about this; the degree of the social price is politically decided, man-made. The technological contribution to human progress can never be a simple gift, but must always exact some price. In brief, technology cannot be amoral.

In the modern world technology is largely the product of our great industrial institutions, a major if not *the* major element of economic life today. It is common knowledge that these institutions have had a long and painful evolution over the past 200 years, an evolution that has been both physically and morally painful. The immense transformation of industrial life from that of the mid-eighteenth century, through the nineteenth with the growth of the factory system which produced both great exploitation of children and also great reforms, to the present day now reads like ancient history. But it is very much a history of moral change. It was Emile Durkheim who observed that whereas in earlier centuries, in pre-industrial times, man's economic activities were subject to and guided by some external, accepted, overriding authority, whether temporal or spiritual (e.g. feudal, military, the Church), which gave these activities meaning and purpose, these authorities ceased to be relevant with the coming of industrialisation.[52] The turning point was, roughly speaking, the time of the French Revolution. The vacuum that was left came to be filled by the state, but very slowly and against fierce opposition, during the nineteenth century. Trade unions were legalised in Britain in 1825, and already there had been parliamentary agitation for state control of the working conditions of children in factories.[53] Unfortunately, these early ideals and reforms were largely ignored by the expanding industry, which accepted no overriding authority, even the state; during the nineteenth century industry became very much an end in itself, an entity with its own rights and largely guided by its own rules; there had ceased to be any overriding authority to give it direction, moral guidance and purpose. In brief, economic life became increasingly secularised,[54] amoral, and rationally directed towards the goal of money. But money is not wealth; wealth is what you do with money. Economics alone can never be a final solution, for that is ultimately a moral matter. In Durkheim's terms economic life, *per se*, has no moral purpose.

The situation today has become somewhat different, and increasingly so since World War II. The vacuum that was left in economic life when the dominant spiritual and temporal powers of earlier centuries ceased to be relevant has steadily and increasingly become filled by the state, in all industrial countries of all political persuasions, through the medium of law. Law and morals are, of course, not to be equated; the law, so long as it is not outdated, does supply some moral guidance, but it involves politics; in Durkheim's words, law is 'the visible symbol' of morality[55] — though, unfortunately, not always a symbol of the current morality in today's fast-changing conditions. Industry since World War II has had to move a little away from being the autonomous power it once was and is increasingly subject to the law, in spite of the steady growth in size of many enterprises. The state has assumed numerous responsibilities which, according to various political beliefs at least have aimed, if not always succeeded, in making our economic life rather more regularised and moralised than hitherto. Through improved rational means — fiscal means, employment regulations, industrial tribunals, consumer protection, grants and subsidies, arbitration during disputes, retirement pension schemes, and in a host of other ways — it has aimed to achieve moral ends.

In the words of my colleague the late Dennis Gabor, writing in his book *Inventing the Future* upon the likely social consequences of unending automation of industry:

> the automatic development of the capitalist system leads to larger and larger (industrial) units — not however to the irresponsible rapacious monopolies which Marx predicated but to large concerns which by their very size are all the time under the watchful

eye of the governments and of the public, and must 'behave themselves' to a degree which would have driven the Victorian entrepreneur to suicide.[56]

Durkheim feared that the state could fail to function as such an overriding authority in a way that would render it able to command the respect of individuals, for it was too awesome and remote. He pressed for the creation of mediating bodies, to come between the individual and the colossus of the state. Today we have a vast array of such intermediary bodies, from the major trade unions to consumer associations — though none of these necessarily corresponds to the particular forms that Durkheim had in mind.[57] All these are in principle subject to the over riding authority of the law, although the majority of them serve the interests of specific groups and maybe none commands the respect of the whole community.

Within those civilised countries which have passed beyond the stage of being ruled by long-established traditions — i.e. are 'developing' — the great protector is assumed to be the law. But under conditions of very rapid technological changes, such as those in industrial countries today, some elements of law are continually outdated as new technologies are created which allow people to act in ways hitherto inconceivable. When the environment changes faster than people themselves are able to, those people will feel threatened. The law is then often not seen as a valid expression of justice and, as Emile Durkheim argued, it is justice that is increasingly needed in our 'changing society' (i.e. society that is continually and compulsively seeking to adapt to a fast-changing environment), just as earlier societies needed a common faith.[58]

This is increasingly true of the 'technology of information', the subject of our book; it was true, in earlier centuries too, because of the special nature of this technology. For example, when the postal service was reorganised in the seventeenth century into a form close to the one we have today (at the time of Oliver Cromwell, in Britain)[59] people were alarmed because, obviously, letters could be opened and people spied upon or blackmailed;[60] so too in the nineteenth century with the coming of the telephone, for speakers could be overheard. The coming of the radio[61] also caused concern, because it was feared as a possible corrupter of people's minds and new law was called for,[62] just as many feel today that television is a threat to their children. Perhaps the most recent example is the computer, which many fear as a means of storing personal records in official files, without right of scrutiny; the law still has this problem to deal with satisfactorily.[63] Again, the duplicating machine has outdated the law of copyright, for whole books may be copied, just as the tape-recorder has done too, for radio programmes and gramophone discs may be copied.

'Broadcast satellites' are another source of worry today because international law has still to reckon with them.[64] The inevitable lag in legal processes, in the face of rapid technological change, is undoubtedly one source of public alarm. The unceasing technological development of the industrial countries has produced sustained stress of social and personal readjustments. The older do not live in quite the same world as the younger, but feel continual challenge to their habits and traditions.

It is these and other contradictions that are built into the concept of 'progress' which so concerned the early social theorists of the nineteenth century, when they saw clearly that the vision of abundance for all, through invention, industry and hard work was a myth and that things seemed to be going wrong.[65] It was perhaps Auguste Comte (1798-1857) who was the chief proponent of the inevitability of 'progress', arguing that man's biological and psychological nature would ensure it.

It may be interesting to note how the word 'progress' has changed its meaning since the seventeenth century. Originally the word simply meant 'a journey'[66] (e.g. Bunyan's *Pilgrim's Progress*)[67] but, subsequent to the work-ethic of Puritanism,[68] it gradually came to mean 'getting better', or 'moving into a better situation'. The coming of the so-called Industrial Revolution[69] in the eighteenth century was not merely the result of a great spurt in inventiveness and financial enterprise, but it meant also a profound change of morals, in social structure and attitudes, and in religious climate.[70]

Thomas Carlyle once referred to 'the three great elements of modern civilisation, Gunpowder, Printing, and the Protestant Religion' — of which, we may notice, two are technological and one is ethical.[71]

This fundamental change in outlook which came about during the eighteenth and nineteenth centuries in the industrialising countries led many people to expect things to get better continually; they had become what in Weberian terms could be called 'goal-seeking societies' — the goal being almost wholly economic. But only if you have set goals or objectives do you have frustrations and disappointments. Even today we still expect things to get better, almost as a right, and we are distressed when they don't; when the GNP does not go on rising, for instance. Few Utopias have been written in the twentieth century.[72]

It is then a great mistake to regard the so-called Industrial Revolution simply as a vast spurt in inventiveness and manufacture, or as the taking over of crafts by machines. Furthermore, it is only too easy to underestimate the extent to which technology existed in medieval times — for stone-cutting and cathedral building, for weaving, watermill and windmill power sources (there were over five thousand mills in England alone in the eleventh century).[73] As Lewis Mumford has said, if we are to think of the progress of technology alone, the Industrial Revolution can be said to have another 700 years of history.[74] The technical origins of our present day 'technological society' are to be found, not in the eighteenth century cottage industries nor in the Renaissance but in medieval times.[75] But we are here thinking of more than technology alone; the social movements which led to the so-called Industrial Revolution may be said to be an outcome of the change in attitude to the world brought about by the Reformation.[76]

If the expression 'a Second Industrial Revolution' can be found to have any meaning it is inadequate to search for this in 'information technology' itself; it requires that some new cause of moral change be sought, or of change in work-ethic, or of change in our 'world view', together with reasons for encouragement of such changes through interaction with the new technology, which we are here calling 'information technology'. It could well be claimed that the 'communication explosion' of the past ten years had indeed compelled an immense change in our world outlook — in greatly increased international awareness, in striving for international order, in ideals and ideologies. Even so, we need to ask the question *Why*? We shall argue here that the technology itself ('information technology') has been a major contributory factor since World War II, for a very special reason. It is technology that is fundamentally different from all others, including transport,[77] being the *technology of sharing*. In principle, (and only in principle) it is technology that handles something abstract (information) which is not a commodity nor can it be 'property' in the conventional sense of that term but, as will be argued next, is something radically new on the scene.

So let us now stop talking about First and Second Industrial Revolutions and look next at these fundamental facts.

6. Communication is Always an Act of Sharing

In a previous book, written in 1957, I pointed out that the word *communication* came from the Latin: *communicare* = to share.[78] It does not mean 'sending messages', for messages cannot possibly be 'sent' in the sense that we speak of sending goods or commodities. Communication is always a social activity, an act of sharing. The reasoning behind this fundamental fact is so crucial to our present study, that it will be repeated here, and expanded upon.

Goods, or commodities, may be exchanged or traded, either by being sold for money or by being bartered for others (Latin: *commutare* = to exchange). The person handing over the goods loses them, and receives money or other goods in exchange. However, the same is not true of messages. If a message is communicated by one person to another, the 'sender' does *not* lose the message — he retains it, either in memory, or even as a duplicate copy. The two people then *both* have it — shared. The word 'sender' is a misnomer. He is really an initiator or a source. Thus, he may send a letter (a commodity), but he shares the message with the recipient. Furthermore, the second person may communicate to a third, so that all three have it, and, if only in principle, that message may be spread throughout the whole of the human race without loss to anyone. That is to say, *it is in the nature of the communication of messages that they are not required to be lost to the source (the initiator), when they are communicated to a receiver.*

However, the word 'sharing' is ambiguous, having two distinct meanings: (a) sharing by division (sharing *between*) as when you share a bar of chocolate with someone and have half each (communication is *not* sharing in this sense); (b) sharing by participation (sharing *with*) as when you hold something in common with others, like the membership of a club, or like having some common interest. Communication means sharing in this latter sense; it is always a social activity.

A good analogy is the spread of an infectious disease; sufferers 'communicate' the infection to others, but do not lose it themselves in the process. The infection may be received, but not sent, just as *messages may be received, but not literally 'sent' in strict contrast to commodities. Messages can only be shared, never exchanged.* In other words, when communicating messages, it *is* possible (indeed, unavoidable) both to have your cake and to eat it too.

A number of conclusions follow from this fact, which are essential to the understanding of what human communication really is. But first, a small point may be cleared up. We must distinguish between the message itself (words on paper, speech, printed texts, etc.) and the meaning of that message. Thus, an identical letter may be circulated to a wide public, or many copies of a book may be sold to readers, but each individual may infer his own peculiar meaning. It is the message itself that is shared; meaning is another matter, which is private to each person and depends upon their experiences and a host of personal factors.

It follows that *messages are not commodities*. They cannot be given away or sold (unless the 'sender' is suddenly struck with loss of memory).[79] Consequently, messages cannot be *property*, in the conventional sense of the word. Of course, a person may withhold some information and refuse to tell others, but it is not his property in the sense of his being able to sell it, or exchange it. He cannot sell his knowledge, in the same way that he can sell his car — i.e. trade it. He cannot even *give* it away. But he may certainly withhold it.

On the other hand, information (facts, data, knowledge) certainly constitutes a *resource*.[80] It may become out of date or otherwise fade in value, but as a resource it is not consumed by usage.

Our argument so far has been that messages (knowledge, information, data, etc.) are not commodities and cannot be exchanged or sold, as such. Furthermore, unlike physical commodities or materials, they are not finite resources, and so have no economic 'scarcity value' imposed by nature. But such argument is idealistic; what actually happens in practice?

Scarcity value can well be given to sources of information by forbidding or constraining their spread, as by man-made law or social custom, thereby bestowing 'economic rarity value' on them in a broad sense of that term. Such constraints may take legal forms of action, such as *censorship* (commercial or political), *security law*, *copyright law*, *patent law*; or simply social custom, as with *privacy*, *confidentiality*, *taboo*, etc.[81]

Essentially, there are three classes of man-made constraint upon the spread of information, corresponding to Max Weber's three classes of possible social action:[82]

(1) *Rational*. ('I cannot tell you because I should lose my job if I did').

(2) *Emotional* (*including moral*). ('I don't like to tell you, because it is so embarrassing').

(3) *Traditional.* ('You don't usually say that sort of thing to children').

It may not be surprising that all such constraints sometimes cause difficulties, or may upset people, because they seek to constrain the spread of information which is something that is not constrained by any natural means, but is indefinitely spreadable. They can be regarded as impositions. People resent censorship, fear security law, are suspicious of confidential reports or letters, are often contemptuous of copyright,[83] whilst today patents are often more commercial bargaining instruments than protectors of the inventor in person. All such constraints may be seen as seeking to treat information or knowledge as a commodity and to impose upon it the old criterion of economic property, which is completely contrary to its real 'shareable' nature.

These points may seem to be no more than philosophic trifles; but they are more. They are of profound importance in today's world of 'haves' and 'have nots'. For the rich industrial countries may, in their seeming generosity, give away goods and commodities to poor countries in programmes of economic aid, but they cannot literally give away any of their vast and accumulating riches of knowledge, factual data or information. They may offer to do so, but this involves them in no sacrifice whatsoever, for they do not lose it in the process. The only 'losses' would be losses of man-made privileges, as claimed by patent law, commercial secrecy, etc.; nature herself imposes no conditions of sacrifice upon a knowledge-rich source when this offers to communicate, and so share, its knowledge with others. It may be argued that this inescapable fact may operate against the interests of the Third World.[84]

We should distinguish between knowledge itself and the power inherent in its possession. Knowledge and information themselves are, in logical principle, shareable among all without loss to any, but their powers may be constrained by man's legal and other devices. Put another way, sources of knowledge and of information are, by nature, bottomless cornucopias; but their outputs may be converted by legal and other man-made devices into 'finite commodities' and thereby given economic rarity value. If knowledge and information from the wealthier countries are to find their way into the poorer countries there will need to come about certain ethical changes in our assumptions of rights over knowledge and information, so that they may be distinguished more clearly from the powers that are at present contained in their retention.[85]

Ralph Waldo Emerson once said: 'invention breeds invention'; the more technology that we have, and understand, the greater is our power for creating yet more. But the analogous problem of today, the information or 'knowledge explosion', raises even more serious question marks. Knowledge, as we have argued here, may be spread but, in so doing, it is not lost to the 'sender'. So we might well parody Emerson by saying that 'knowledge breeds knowledge'. The more we know, the more can be learned; knowledge is both accumulative and accelerating, and concentrated at those centres where it may be accumulated — in libraries, computers, data-banks — that is, in wealthier countries, where it is not only stored, but also created.

What can constrain this accumulation, or is it conceivable that its expansion will continue forever without check? The first thing that springs to mind is, of course, the problem of accessibility — how to locate the information when it is needed and *within the time that it is available for its practical use.* Computers are fast being introduced into libraries and elsewhere to help with this problem; but they cannot alone solve the problem. The ultimate limitation lies in people's heads. The more we know, the more we realise the complexity of so many of today's practical problems, and the more we realise we need to know more, in order to deal with them. We become more critical. In government, and in all high places, decision-making becomes increasingly complex and involves increasing scientific and technical knowledge. Whereas in earlier times one senior person could make decisions, he later needed advisors, and then, later still, advisory committees. The whole 'bureaucratic' structure (the information sector) must grow in scale and in ability as 'the knowledge explosion' continues, if we or our descendants are to deal with the future national and international problems, as this knowledge increasingly both reveals their complexities and provides us with more complex methods for attacking them. As in Section 3 we use the term 'bureaucracy' here in its literal, non-perjorative sense to mean the administrative, organisational elements of government. The forms of 'bureaucracy' which we have inherited seem well on their way to becoming outdated, as decision-making increasingly depends upon expertise, of widening range, and upon speed of action.

In his book *The Changing Information Environment* John McHale has written:[86]

The new information environment creates new forms of 'property'. . . . It may tend to create a new and powerful 'property class', whose property is in their heads — those exclusively possessing the specific skills required for access to, and manipulation of, vital knowledge and information.

The quotes placed here about the word 'property' are important. Strictly, the power of knowledge is not the power of property-ownership, such as that of land or goods. I would not disagree at all with the tenor of McHale's comment, but only with his use of the word 'property'.

To speak of communication as 'sharing', or as a social act (indeed the primary social act) should not mislead us into thinking that communication necessarily 'brings people together' — for it can equally well drive them apart.[87] We may agree or disagree, be friendly or quarrel. Communication may lead either to co-operation or to competition. Communication may unite us or divide us — an idea that goes back to Aristotle.[88] And division is important, for it is essentially division, dissent, disagreement, that is the source of social change; mere continued unquestioning agreement, total conformity, by itself would produce paralysis.

Whereas all goods, materials, commodities etc. are ultimately in finite supply on this earth, messages need not be, for they can, if only in principle, spread indefinitely as we have already argued — unless something is done to prevent this happening. As we have seen, this is exactly what is done, by man-made constraints. For otherwise messages would have no *economic scarcity value*, as material goods have, by nature. The economic principles of operating all our various communication and information services must differ radically from the economic principles of trade and exchange of goods. We all know how difficult it is to place an equitable price on knowledge,[89] for it is not a commodity that is saleable. You do not part with your knowledge when you impart it to others. They may gain by it, but you do not (indeed cannot) lose it.

The economics of the telephone service or of computer usage, or of other information services, are therefore likely to be very different from the economic principles of trade and exchange. Such studies as have been done, do indeed suggest this (including principles of equitable user tariff systems).[90,91] The economic principles of 'sharing' are likely to differ widely from those of exchange.

To me it seems extraordinary that neither sociologists nor economists have shown much interest in the various communication or information services, a fact that certain of them have remarked upon.[92] One reason may be that the various economic institutions of industrial countries have evolved over centuries upon the principle of *exchange* — either of trade, or barter, or plunder — in competition for the finite material resources of the world. On the other hand, the various national and inter-national communication services, which are expanding in a way that we have called 'explosive', are of relatively recent origin.[93] Being based upon the principle of *sharing* their significance to economic theory requires radical rethinking. This seems to be a very serious lacuna in the social sciences, as both national and international economic life are today utterly dependent upon communication and information services. To quote Ronald Stamper of the London School of Economics: 'Economics has practically no place for information in its analyses except to assume that information is readily available to the decision-maker.'[94]

Another reason for the comparative lack of economic study on the values of information services may be that they contribute to economic life in two, quite different, ways which are sometimes confused. First, there is the contribution by the equipment manufacturing industries directly — e.g. the electronics industry, computer manufacturers, the telephone industry, etc. These are manufacturing industries, like any others, using raw materials and producing equipment for sale and export. Similarly the press uses paper and ink, manufacturing newspapers, books etc. as objects for sale. Secondly, there is the economic value deriving from the messages (information) which they enable us to share. It is only this second contribution to economic life that concerns us here — what has been termed its *organisational value*, which stems from the principle of 'sharing'. Thus, the telephone service, computer services, the familiar postal service, data transmission, 'electronic mail' and all the other information services enable business, industry, banking, scheduled transport, and all the other organised economic institutions of industrial countries to operate, including government itself. They may be regarded as extensions of the early traditions of good accountancy and record-keeping that helped to facilitate the Industrial Revolution in the eighteenth century. It is all these information services which make possible the highly rational, organised, 'bureaucratic' element of industrial society, as described in Section 3. They operate upon the principle of 'sharing' and not that of 'exchange'.

Transport services, such as railways and airways, are often referred to as 'communication services', particularly in the military sphere. Strictly speaking, they are not,[95] because they use the principle of *exchange*. They are better called *commutation* services (Latin: *commutare* = to exchange). When travelling, you cannot be at both ends of the line at the same time, whereas when telephoning your voice literally does achieve that feat. You are, in voice and mind, at both locations simultaneously. When communicating (as, say, by telephone) you are both here *and* there; it is essentially a social activity. But when travelling you are here *or* there; transport itself is not a social experience (although conversation on the journey certainly is!).

It will be argued in Chapter 2 that, for this and other reasons, telecommunication cannot wholly substitute for travel, but that, on the contrary, expansion of the world's telecommunication services (including 'tele-conferencing') is more likely to encourage increase in personal travel, as it always has done in the past.[96]

Notes

1. See 'Men, Machines and their Interconnections', Sir Edmund Leach — an Open University/British Association paper, read before the British Association meeting, September 1977 (unpublished).

2. See *Objective Knowledge: an Evolutionary Approach*, K. Popper, Oxford University Press, London, 1972,1975; Also, *Popper* by B. Magee, Fontana paperbacks, London, 1973.

3. See *Technics and Civilisation*, L. Mumford, Harcourt Brace Jovanovich, New York, and Routledge & Kegan Paul, London, 1934. *Cybernetics*, N. Wiener, The Technology Press, John Wiley & Sons Inc., New York, and Herman et Cie, Paris, 1948. 'Tools or Toys? (What have we really learned from wild chimpanzees about tool usage?)' Kitahara-Frisch, *Journal of the Anthropological Society of Nippon, 85 (1)*, March 1977, 57 ff.

4. See note 18.

5. See *A History of the Marconi Company*, W.J. Baker, Methuen & Co. Ltd, London, 1970. *Marconi (a biography)*, W.P. Jolly, Constable, London, 1972.

6. Hertz's letter, stating this opinion, is held in the Deutsche Museum, Munich, and is reproduced in *Invention and Innovation in the Radio Industry*, W.R. Maclaurin, Macmillan, London, 1949, and in *Pioneers of Electrical Communications*, R. Appleyard, Macmillan, London, 1930.

7. See 'Radio Communication by Means of Very Short Electric Waves', G. Marconi, *Proceedings of the Royal Institution, Great Britain, 1932, 27*, 509-44. Reprinted in *Institute of Radio Engineers Transactions on Antennas and Propagation, vol. AP5*, January 1957, 90-9. 'Marconi's Last Paper, "On the Propagation of Microwaves over Considerable Distances" ', T.J. Carroll, *Proceedings of the*

Institute of Radio Engineers, 44 (8), August 1956. Also, 'The Spirit of Discovery; An Appreciation of the Work of Marconi', E.H. Armstrong, *Elec. Eng., 72*, August 1953, 670-6.

8. Karl Popper argued that if the results of an experiment support someone's theory it does not prove that theory to be correct; it merely gives evidence that it might be so. On the other hand, if the results disagree with the theory, that theory must be wrong in some way. Science does not work by discovering 'truth' but by systematic detection of error. See B. Magee, *Popper* (note 2).

9. For example, some chimpanzees may deliberately break off a small tree branch and use it for grubbing out insects, etc., for scaring predators, etc. However, such uses of tools may be more akin to 'hobbies' or pastimes. See Kitahara-Frisch (note 3). See note 16. See also, *Man the Tool Maker*, Phoenix Books, University of Chicago Press, 1959, and 'A Definition of Man', *Penguin Science News, No. 20*, Harmondsworth, UK, 1951 — both by K. Oakley.

10. See *Emile Durkheim (Life and Thought)*, R. Bierstedt, Weidenfeld & Nicholson, London, 1966, 1969.

11. Thomas Carlyle once wrote: 'Man is a Tool-using Animal. . . Feeblest of bipeds!. . . Nevertheless he can use Tools, can devise Tools:. . . Nowhere do you find him without Tools; without Tools he is nothing, with Tools he is all.' (*Sartor Resartus*, Book i, Chapter 5; *The World in Clothes*, published in 1838). See also *Suicide: a Study in Sociology*, E. Durkheim, (translated by A. Spaulding and G. Simpson), G. Simpson (ed.), Macmillan Publishing Co. Inc., New York, and Routledge & Kegan Paul Ltd, London, 1952, (first published, in French, in 1897). *Main Currents in Sociological Thought*, Volume 1 (Montesquieu, Comte, Tocqueville, Marx), Volume 2 (Durkheim, Pareto, Weber), both by R. Aron, Weidenfeld & Nicholson, London 1968, (and Basic Books Inc., New York).

12. [A matter to have been discussed further in Chapter 6.] See 'The Study of Man in Relation to Science and Technology'; two Cantor Lectures: (i) 'Technological Progress and Cultural Variety', (ii) 'Has Science Had a History?' Sir Edmund Leach, *Journal of the Royal Society of Arts*, London, June 1973.

13. See the Durkheim reference in note 11, especially Book 3, Chapter 1, p. 313.

14. See the previous note, and R. Aron (note 11).

15. [In the file of notes for Chapter 2 Cherry placed a scrap of manuscript originally intended for Chapter 1, discarded, and subsequently used in part, in Chapter 1. It reads:

. . . wild nature, but one that has been licked into shape, in different ways, in various parts of the world; it is largely 'man-made'. The fields, the hedgerows, the towns and cities, the railways and airways are just as much social facts as are the baked mud or wooden huts of the most primitive villages. We make our environment with the technology, the tools, that we happen to possess. And in Durkheim's terms these then 'give definite direction' to our activities.

However, such a phrase must be interpreted carefully. The specific technological environment in which any of us live does not decide precisely what our activities shall be. Rather it offers us what might be termed specific 'liberties of action' (or 'degrees of freedom of action')*. Thus, when any new invention appears there is no way of telling exactly how it will be used, within a given community, but only the general types of action that it offers.

---

* In the manuscript the word 'powers' is shown crossed out and replaced by the word 'liberties'. It is curious to find Cherry obviously fishing for the phrase 'liberties of action'. This is especially so when it is so memorable and so apposite, and when, in fact, he had used it before. The following passage is taken from his paper 'The Telephone System: Creator of Mobility and Social Change'. (See notes 46 and 22.)

Inventions themselves are not revolutions; neither are they the cause of revolutions. Their powers for change lie in the hands of those who have the imagination and insight to see that the new invention has offered them new liberties of action, that old constraints have been removed, that their political will, or their sheer greed, are no longer frustrated, and that they can act in new ways. New social behaviour patterns and new social institutions are created which in turn become the commonplace experience of future generations.

Such realization does not come easily, quickly, or even 'naturally', for the new invention can first be seen by society only in terms of the liberties of action it currently possesses. We say society is 'not ready', meaning that it is bound by its present customs and habits to think in terms of its existing institutions. Realization of new liberties, and creation of new institutions means social change, new thought, and new feelings. The invention alters the society, and eventually is used in ways that were at first quite unthinkable.

[See also Chapter 2, Sections 2 and 5.]

16. Koehler made extensive observation of what appeared to be tool-making and tool using by chimpanzees, in East Africa some sixty years ago, but, as Kitahara-Frisch has pointed out, he recommended 'great prudence in interpreting the function of tool behaviour in chimpanzees'. The latter, he felt, 'may often be closer to play than to the performance of a task'. Kitahara-Frisch advises us that the same comments are valid today; the values of these activities seems more to be for mental development in chimpanzees; toys rather than tools serve similar functions in children. See note 9. See Kitahara-Frisch (note 3). See *The Mentality of Apes*, W. Koehler, Routledge & Kegan Paul, London, 1925.

17. See *A History of Science*, Sir William C. Dampier, Cambridge University Press, UK, 1948.

18. [This point was to have been taken up in Chapter 6.]

19. In the words of Lewis Munford: 'the essential distinction between a machine and a tool lies in the degree of independence in the operation from the skill and motive power of the operator: the tool lends itself to manipulation, the machine to automatic action'. Extracted from the book *Technics and Civilisation*, (see note 3 for bibliographic details). However, this distinction does not enter into any of the arguments in this book; hence the general word artefact will be used most commonly. See also note 16 for distinction between tools and toys.

20. [This was to have been discussed in Chapter 8.]

21. See *English Social History*, G.M. Trevelyan, Longmans, Green & Co., London, 1942, and L. Mumford (note 3).

22. Born 130 BC, Hero invented two types of 'steam engines'; one was his well-known reaction turbine, whilst the other, using the heat of a fire lit on the altar in a temple, was actually used to open the temple doors. (See *Encyclopaedia Brittanica* under 'Steam Engine'). Many inventions of recent centuries too were first regarded as toys, including the telephone. See 'The Pleasure Telephone: A Chapter in the Pre-history of the Media', by Lord Asa Briggs, in the volume *The Social Impact of the Telephone*, Ithiel de Sola Pool (ed.), MIT Press, Cambridge, Mass., and London, UK, 1977.

23. 'Government by officials' (*The Concise Oxford English Dictionary*, 1976 edition).

24. That is to say, 'bureaucracy' under the law. This essentially implies a continuing administrative structure of qualified officials, whose relationships, duties, rights and responsibilities are defined by law; these officials operate as functionaries, on an impersonal basis, and they do not own the resources needed for execution of their tasks. Their business is based upon written documents or other permanent records. See *The Theory of Social and Economic Organisation*, (with an Introduction by Talcott Parsons), Max Weber, Oxford University Press, New York,

Inc., 1947, and the Free Press, New York. *Max Weber (an Intellectual Portrait)*, R. Bendix, Methuen & Co. Ltd, London, 1966 (USA 1959); R. Aron (note 11).

25. See 'Formal Information Systems — Their Role in the Economy and in Society', R.K. Stamper, in *Computers and People*, Parkin (ed.), Edward Arnold, London, 1977. (Proceedings of a Conference on Computers and People, held at Leicester Polytechnic, December 1976). *The Changing Information Environment*, J. McHale, Paul Elek, London, 1976.

26. 'Rational' in the sense of 'according to rules', using established, defined, codes of practice.

27. See *The Protestant Ethic and the Spirit of Capitalism*, Max Weber, translated by Talcott Parsons, Allen & Unwin, London, 1930, and Scribner & Sons, New York, 1958. First published as an essay entitled 'Die Protestantische Ethik und der Geist des Kapitalismus', in *Archiv für Sozialwissenschaft und Sozialpolitic*, Volumes XX and XXI, 1904-5. It was reprinted with considerable changes and extensive footnotes in *Gesammelte Aufsätze zur Religionssociologie*, in 1920 (not completed at his death). See also R. Aron (note 11), and R. Bendix (note 24). [Possibly also, (his footnote here had a '?'), *Religion and the Rise of Capitalism*, R.H. Tawney, Penguin Books, London, 1938.]

28. [The Bill was implemented on 1 January 1947. Cherry gave the date for the debate as 20 May 1946. However, he seems to have been in error. Hansard reveals (Column 828, 29/1/46) that Jennie Lee said, to Mr Thorneycroft, during the Coal Industry Nationalisation Bill debate: Would the hon. Gentleman tell me what he proposes to do if the miners refuse his terms? Has he not realised yet that the miner has the whip hand? Hansard also reveals (Column 1217, 2/4/46) that Sir Hartley Shawcross said, during the debate on the Trade Disputes and Trade Unions Bill: We are the masters at the moment, and not only at the moment, but for a very long time to come . . . The *Oxford Dictionary of Quotations* (revised edition, 1980) says of this quotation that it is 'often misquoted as "We are the masters now".']

29. [More was to have been said about this subject later, in Chapters 6, 7 and 8.]

30. Except in a certain existential sense; it exerts power *over* those who possess it. This point will be raised again in Chapter 2.

31. See J. McHale (note 25). *The Coming of Post Industrial Society*, D. Bell, Basic Books, New York, 1973; *The Production and Distribution of Knowledge in the United States*, F. Machlup, Princeton University Press, Princeton, 1962; 'Social Implications of Computer/Telecoms Systems', E.B. Parker, *Telecommunication Policy, 1 (1)*, December 1976, 3. *Inventing the Future*, D. Gabor. Martin Secker & Warburg, London, and Alfred Knopf Inc., New York, 1963.

32. D. Bell (note 31).

33. I am indebted to Professor Rupert Hall for advice on this point. See also *Lectures on the Industrial Revolution of the Eighteenth Century in England*, A. Toynbee, Longmans, Green & Co., 1916, and other editions. First published in 1884.

34. For example, the Royal Society of Arts, founded in Britain in 1754, still has the full title: 'The Royal Society for the Encouragement of Arts, Manufactures and Commerce'.

35. [To have been done in Chapter 7.]

36. See *The Idea of Progress (An Enquiry Into its Origins and Growth)'*, J.B. Bury, Dover Publications Inc., New York, 1932.

37. See E.B. Parker (note 31). J. McHale (note 25). F. Machlup (note 31). Also 'Common Carrier Telecommunications in the World Economy', *Telecommunications Journal*, October 1972, and 'Telephony is a Heavy Industry', *Telecommunications Journal*, October 1975, both by R.J. Chapuis; and 'Technology and Structures — Man and Machine', by R.J. Chapuis, in *Evaluating New Telecommunications Services*, M.C.J. Elton, W.A. Lucas and D.W. Conrath (eds), Plenum Press, New York and London, 1978.

38. See J. McHale (note 25).

39. See *Basic Human Needs*, J. McHale and M.C. McHale, Transaction Books, New Jersey, 1978 (a Report to the UN Environment Programme, April 1977). *The Sane Alternative*, J. Robertson, published by James Robertson, 7 St Ann's Villas, London, W11 4RU, 1978, (Villiers Publications Ltd, London).

40. E.B. Parker (note 31), refers to 'The Information Economy', M. Porat, unpublished PhD dissertation, Institute for Communication Research, Stanford University, California, 1976.

41. US Bureau of Labour.

42. Proceedings of the OECD Conference on Computer/Telecommunication Policy, 4-6 February, 1975. OECD Informatics Studies No. 11, Pan Books 1976.

43. M. Porat (note 40). F. Machlup (note 31).

44. E.B. Parker (note 31).

45. See *Computers, Office Machines and the New Information Technology*, C. Hegel, Macmillan, London, 1969. J. McHale (note 25).

46. See 'The Telephone System: Creator of Mobility and Social Change', E.C. Cherry, in the volume by I.de Sola Pool (note 22).

47. See *The Rules of Sociological Method*, E. Durkheim, (translated by S.A. Solovay, J.H. Mueller), G.E.G. Cattin (ed.), Macmillan, London, and the Free Press, New York, 1966. (First published in French in 1895). Also, R. Bierstedt (note 10).

48. Human artefacts may broadly be divided into two classes (a) 'Toys' (objects employed for self gratification or self-development) and (b) 'Tools' (objects used for specific tasks). See Kitahara-Frisch (note 3); (see notes 9 and 16). See E. Durkheim (note 11), R. Aron (note 11).

49. The reader's attention is drawn to the profusely illustrated volume edited by Lord Asa Briggs entitled *The 19th Century; the Contradictions of Progress*, Thames & Hudson, London, 1970.

50. See *A Study of History*, A.J. Toynbee, abridged edition by D.C. Somervel, Oxford University Press, London, 1946. *The New Industrial State*, J.K. Galbraith, Hamish Hamilton, London, 1967. *Machines — Masters or Slaves of Man?* M. Thring, Peter Peregrinus, Stevenage, Great Britain, 1973.

51. See A.J. Toynbee (note 50). *Sociologism & Existentialism*, A. Tiryakian, Prentice Hall, London, 1962.

52. See *The Division of Labour in Society*, E. Durkheim, (translated by G. Simpson), Macmillan, London, and the Free Press, New York, 1933. (First published, in French, in 1893).

53. G.M. Trevelyan (note 21).

54. M. Weber (note 24).

55. E. Durkheim (note 52).

56. D. Gabor (note 31).

57. E. Durkheim (note 52). See the Preface to the second edition, and also p. 358 et seq. of that book.

58. E. Durkheim (note 52).

59. By Act of Parliament dated 1657.

60. At the time of Oliver Cromwell, who was Protector, responsibility for inland and foreign mail was naturally assumed by Parliament, which regarded the postal service both as a source of revenue and as a means of political espionage. Private mail couriers were trampled down by Cromwell's soldiery. (See *Encyclopaedia Brittanica* under 'Post').

61. See volume 1 of *The History of Broadcasting in the United Kingdom*, Lord Asa Briggs, published in 3 volumes by Oxford University Press, London; *The Birth of Broadcasting* (1961), *The Golden Age of Wireless* (1965), *The War of Words* (1970).

62. In Britain the Sykes Committee was set up to consider the whole set of problems raised by the new 'wireless' (radio) including legal aspects, censorship, ownership,

public and governmental control, advertising, license evasion, public controversy, etc. See *The Broadcasting Committee Report 1923*, Sir Frederik Sykes, HMSO London, 1923.

63. [References were 'still to be found' for this point.]

64. To be discussed further in Chapter 2. See also 'Feasibility of Direct Sound and Television Broadcasting from Satellites', CCIR Report No. 215, (Xth Plenary Assembly of the Comité Consultatif International de Radiodiffusion, Geneva, 1963).

65. R. Aron (note 11). L. Mumford (note 3). G.M. Trevelyan (note 21).

66. Particularly a royal journey (e.g. 'The Queen's Progress'). The word retains its early meaning today sometimes, as when we see a notice pinned on the door of a conference room saying 'A Meeting is in Progress' — which does not mean that the meeting is actually getting anywhere!

67. Published in 1678. Strictly, Bunyan used the word to mean a pilgrimage — a journey undertaken lovingly, with a sense of duty, but not in the sense of getting *better* or improving one's lot.

68. [A subject to have been taken up in Chapter 7.]

69. In England this is usually taken to be the mid-18th century, though there had been essential conditions building up long before. Thus, capitalism, factories and overseas trade were part of the English scene long before the year 1750, and the foundations of trade unionism were laid (albeit illegally).

70. For example, the flourishing of Methodism, which was so responsible for educational, medical and other social reforms and in which the Laity played such an active part. See G.M. Trevelyan (note 21).

71. See 'The State of German Literature', Thomas Carlyle, 1827, published in *Critical & Miscellaneous Essays*, volume 1, Chapman & Hall, 1872.

72. D. Gabor (note 31).

73. As recorded in the *Doomsday Book*; the population of England was then probably about 2 million. See *The Medieval Machine*, J. Gimpel, Victor Gollancz Ltd, London, 1977.

74. L. Mumford (note 3).

75. See *Man and Technics*, O. Spengler, Alfred A. Knopf, (Borzoi Books), New York, 1932. L. Mumford (note 3).

76. [To have been discussed in Chapter 7.]

77. Transport is often spoken of as 'communication', especially in military circles, but as we shall see in the following Section this is a misconception (see also Section 8 of Chapter 2).

78. See *On Human Communication*, E.C. Cherry, MIT Press. The text of Section 6 here is adapted from that of Chapter 8, Section (1) of the third edition (1978) of this book. The argument was also given in a paper delivered to the World Telecommunications Forum, 1975. See 'On the Political Nature of World Telecommunication', E.C. Cherry, International Telecommunications Union, (Telecommunications Forum, 6 October 1975, plenary session), Geneva. Also, 'Communication: some Contradictions, Dilemmas and Dangers', E.C. Cherry, proceedings of the conference on 'Cost Conscious Communications', Institute of Administrative Management, Beckenham, Kent, UK, 24 November 1975.

79. Of course, messages may be passed from a 'sender' by an intermediary, perhaps in cypher. That intermediary (e.g. the postman) is not communicating the message. To him it is merely a commodity (a 'vehicle').

80. It was Thomas Hobbes who wrote: 'Knowledge is power' (*Leviathan*, Chapter 9).

81. See the three references detailed in note 78.

82. M. Weber (note 24), R. Aron (note 11).

83. Copyright law has become completely outdated by modern duplicating machines. Why should students (or professors for that matter) buy books, when

duplicating them is cheaper, 'strictly for private use'?

84. [This point was to have been taken up in Chapter 8.]

85. 'But this takes us into Chapter 8'.

86. J. McHale (note 25).

87. R. Aron (note 11).

88. E. Durkheim (note 52); R. Bierstedt (note 10).

89. This problem arises today through the widespread and increasing usage of public libraries. How should the author be recompensed? By a levy on borrowing perhaps? His royalties do not depend upon the borrowings at present.

90. For example, when a telephone call is made it is usually the initiator of the call who pays. But why should this be assumed to be equitable, on all occasions? Calls are frequently made for the receiver's benefit (the 'transferred charge' rule pays some concession to this). Neither partner is 'buying' or 'selling' anything to one another. They are merely paying rent for their use of the telephone equipment.

91. Over a wide range of the world's telephone services it has been shown that the ratio:

$$\frac{\text{invested capital in plant}}{\text{gross annual revenue}} = 3 \text{ (approximately)}$$

which has been called Huntley's Law, whereas over a wide range of productive industries:

$$\frac{\text{invested capital in plant}}{\text{gross annual revenue}} = \frac{1}{3} \text{ (approximately)}$$

so that:

$$\frac{\text{invested (fixed) capital in telecommunication}}{\text{invested (fixed) capital in industry}}$$

for a given return, is a very large ratio — probably approaching 10 to 1. Admittedly these figures must be very approximate, but at least it is clear that telecommunication is an extremely capital-intensive business. It is also true that, in the UK at least and most likely in other countries, the Post Office is the largest single employer (including the postal service). Enormous investment must be made by any industrial country in its telecommunication plant, which must have long life, and this investment must necessarily be amortised over a very long period of time. Chapius has examined some of the socio-economic argument behind Huntley's Law. See, in connection with the above, the three references given in note 37 to work by R.J. Chapius; also, 'Some Ideas Regarding Economics of Telecommunications Engineering', H.R. Huntley, *Electrical Communication, 42 (1),* 1967. 'Telecommunications Market Demand and Investment Requirements', L.L. Bower, *Telecommunications Journal,* 39 (111), 1972.

92. An exception is television (which is strictly a unilateral, dissemination, service and not a communication service). To the best of the writer's knowledge only one major book has appeared in the past 100 years on the sociology of the telephone (see I. de Sola Pool (note 22)). Also, J.M. Clarke pointed out, in 1927, that 'knowledge is the only instrument of production that is not subject to diminishing returns'. (From 'Overhead Costs and Modern Industry', *Journal of Political Economics,* October 1927). See also, R.K. Stamper (note 25).

93. For example, see E.C. Cherry *World Communication: Threat or Promise?,* John Wiley & Son, UK and New York, 1971, (revised 1978). This contains some typical growth curves.

94. R.K. Stamper (note 25).

95. It has to be noted, nevertheless, that the railways and airways and all other scheduled transport services are utterly dependent upon communication services for their running to schedules, for their security, etc., i.e. for their running *as organised services*.

96. See Chapter 2, Section 8; also, E.C. Cherry (note 93).

2 ON THE SOCIO-POLITICAL[1] NATURE OF TECHNOLOGY

> The end of a man is an action, and not a thought, though it were the noblest. (Thomas Carlyle), *Sartor Resartus*, Book ii, Chapter 6.

1. A Technology is Meaningful Only in a Social Context

In a fascinating series of short television broadcasts made in 1976, entitled 'It's Patently Obvious', the BBC introduced a novel form of guessing game.[2] A small panel of (highly educated) people was shown various artefacts from earlier centuries, which had been borrowed from museums, and invited to judge what the purposes of these objects had been. They could handle and manipulate them but, even so, the task often seemed to present great difficulty.

One example might be mentioned here. This consisted of a pair of long tongs, made of steel and highly decorated, with a whistle incorporated in one of the handles. What could this possibly have been used for? Another question could well be put to yourself: If you had this object in your home, what could you use it for today?

From its appearance and the style of the decoration, this pair of tongs was correctly judged to have come from the late eighteenth centure (an artistic, not a technical judgement). Hence, one could imagine something about the historical and social environment in which it was used. But what was the whistle for? Summoning servants? If so, it would not have been used in the home; servants were summoned by bell-pulls, with the bell in the kitchen and peace and quiet in the parlour. Obviously, the environment must have been a noisy one. . .got it? Yes — in an eighteenth-century coffee house. Such devices were called 'ember tongs', and people used them for lighting their long clay pipes ('churchwardens') from hot embers as they sat in front of the fire, and whistled above the din for some tobacco.

Whilst watching this television programme it was interesting for one to note that the people poring over these objects, frowning and muttering as they struggled to guess, would ask for clues to help them, and that so often the help they needed was social or historical in character and not technical. They needed to establish the approximate date, for example, or the social situation in which the objects were used — was it domestic, military, industrial, whilst travelling, etc.? Having got this evidence, they would rapidly converge on to the correct answer concerning the original purpose of the artefact.

This exercise made one essential fact about technology surprisingly clear, namely, that a technological artefact does not by itself, reveal its own purpose. Put another way, a technological artefact has no specific meaning outside a social context. Alone it is dead-metal; it is the social situation that gives it a particular significance.

Significance is one thing; value is another. The value of some technological artefact is not inherent in the object itself but, like its meaning or significance its value depends upon the user, in his particular social context. But what enables that person to place a value upon it? Although he was not specifically considering techno-logical artefacts but values in general, Emile Durkheim[3] argued that human beings are able to place a value on something (economic, moral, religious, aesthetic or speculative value) only because they are able to create ideals. Further, that such ideals are distinct from the realities, being outside and 'above' them, and that the source of these ideals is society itself — the social groups into which that person was born and bred. Consequently, the value of any par-ticular artefact will vary among different social groups and peoples of different social conditions. It further follows that, as a society comes to acquire more and more things, to become more and more a 'technological society' or an 'acquisitive society' (which is not the same), or merely a wealthier society, its nature changes, and so its ideals and its morals are subject to change too. Any political moves made by Governments aimed at raising economic or industrial standards, are then not only seen to have material objectives but essentially moral ones too — not only by those enjoying the rising standards, but perhaps even more by those who are being left out.

These same ideas may be transferred to the present day, as when some radically new invention appears 'before society is ready for it'. But before doing this, we should be careful to distinguish between an *invention* and an *improvement*. Thus, if we were to examine all the patents that there are we might find that the bulk of them repre-sent improvements of something that has existed before; the new one may be faster in operation, more universal, cheaper, easier to maintain, or, very likely, merely a way of avoiding the constraints of somebody else's patent. Such novelties do not introduce radically new concepts. The public would recognise them and have a good chance of imagining their uses and values. Only rarely does some radically new *invention* appear for which there is no existing prototype, and upon which no existing social institutions depend. An obvious example is the aircraft, which is not merely an improvement over the railway train, or a better kind of automobile. Certainly, many people had previously imagined the possibility of human flight, but this had no effect upon the operation of their social lives: it was the appearance of aircraft in reality that led to the creation of new forms of social institution and styles of social behaviour.[4]

Sir Edmund Leach has observed that most of the radically new inventions which have appeared since the year 1780 have introduced new forms of 'communication at a distance', citing as examples: the telegraph, the telephone, radio, television, multi-access computers, together with railways, aeroplanes, motor transport, and others.[5] However, for the purpose of this book we must distinguish between *communication* and *transportation*. Certainly, both are action at a distance but, as was argued in Chapter 1, they introduce quite different principles into the organisation of social life. To remind the reader[6] communication, with its technology, operates upon the principle of *sharing*, (by participation), whilst transportation operates upon the principle of *exchange*; we should therefore expect their social outcomes to differ in certain respects. For example, when telephoning you are, both in voice and mind, at both ends at once — here *and* there; but when travelling by train you are not — you are here *or* there. For this reason we shall here preserve this distinction between communication and transportation.

Let us return now to the point raised two paragraphs back concerning the appearance of a radically new invention 'before society is ready for it' — but with the invention of communication systems particularly in mind. We had been arguing there that, just as it is difficult to guess the uses to which certain very novel artefacts of earlier centuries were put or what significance or values they offered (without knowledge of the social or historical environments), so it is also difficult, if not well-nigh impossible, to guess what will be the future uses, significance, and values of radically new inventions of our own day — especially those pertaining to human communication. The reasons are very similar, namely, that we do not know what will be the social conditions of the future, what will be the new customs and habits, the new institutions, the political and economic changes.

When any new invention appears people can see it at first only in terms of their existing customs and habits; at least that is so with the majority of the population. Few people have the insight, or the powers of imagination, to see that the new invention has presented them with totally new 'liberties of action', or that it has removed old constraints upon certain actions and that society can now organise and act in new ways. New social behaviour patterns and new social institutions may eventually be created which, in their turn, become the commonplace experiences of future generations. When the invention first appears, if it is really radically new, we may say that 'society is not ready', by which we mean that its people are so bound by their present customs and habits that they can think, act and feel only according to their existing social expectations. Eventually, the invention leads to changes in the society, and it comes into uses which were at first totally unthinkable.[7]

It is therefore not always correct to say that if some new invention proves to be economically successful and to sell well, then it has 'satisfied a demand'. For if the invention is something that is at first totally beyond the conceptions of the public, there cannot be said to be a demand — 'the market' does not exist. It is rather that the appearance of the new invention has come to *create* a new market. Indeed, it is a fair judgement that all truly radical new inventions come eventually to be used for purposes which are totally different from anything that the public, or even the inventor himself, could at first imagine.

Let us next consider two examples, both of which have had the profoundest effects upon the organisation of our economic life and may have even greater consequences in store for the world in the future: the telephone and the computer.

2. Telephones and Computers: the Unpredictable Outcomes of Radical Inventions

The telephone is something that is so familiar to us today, so much a part of the everyday scene, whether in home, office or factory, that we take it for granted. It is virtually impossible for us to imagine what life was like in industrial countries before its appearance in the year 1876 and its subsequent very rapid adoption, or how people thought and felt or planned their affairs. It is similarly easy to overlook our utter dependence today upon the telephone service, national and international, for the operations of our social organisations — in industry, business, government, news services, transport services, police, security — an endless list. The telephone service has been a prerequisite for the evolution of our present-day forms of 'bureaucratic'[8] industrialised societies, just as it will be a prerequisite for social and economic development in Third World countries. So it is rather surprising to see how relatively little attention sociologists have given to the subject.[9]

We may therefore find it amusing to read of the uses which the people of 1876 imagined for their new toy, the 'Speaking Telephone'. For that was how it appeared to them — it seemed to have no immediate, useful, function in their society, any more than did Hero's turbine steam engine have for the Alexandrians in the first century BC, and for similar reasons, namely that 'society was not ready'.

Neither, apparently, was Sir William Preece, the Chief Engineer of the British Post Office, when he reported to tne House of Commons in 1879 that there was little need for the new invention in Britain. His words have gone down in history: 'Here we have a superabundance of messengers, errand boys and things of that kind. . .if I want to send a message — I use a sounder or employ a boy to take it'. The telephone was no more than a toy when Graham Bell first demonstrated it to the public,[10] an amusing and entertaining diversion. Some people of religious sensibility were actually offended by it, for the idea of a machine speaking like a human was an offence in the sight of God.

It should be remembered that the first demonstration by Bell used the telephone unilaterally, from the speaker to a listener, who could not reply. It thus became obvious that it could be used as a better kind of speaking-tube for sending orders to servants.[11] This use was advertised in the press of the day; for example, in 1878 the *Journal of the Telegraph Electrical Society of Melbourne*, published two advertisements.[12] The first of these shows a picture of the new 'articulating telephone' with, alongside, a picture of an electric bell and hotel room-indicator — the advertisement then explains the superiority of the telephone over the old bell-pull, saying 'all pulling, tugging and the grating noises occasioned by the cranks, and consequent breaking of the wires are done away with'. The second advertisement shows a Victorian-looking man speaking over the wire to a woman, whilst the wording of the advertisement proposes several uses for the new invention all of which suggest master/servant relationships (e.g. between principals and employees, between central and branch banks, between managers in coalmines and the miners at the face, between 'the superintendent and his leading men').

The article in this early Australian journal makes an interesting sociological study, and perhaps one quotation may be permitted here. Describing the novel experience of using the new 'articulating telephone', the writer says: 'Everyone around should be perfectly quiet. . .the sound comes in a singularly weird-like manner. . .when a ghostly "co-o-o-e" is heard, coming from fifty or a hundred miles away, the receiver is almost awe-struck'. The writer goes on to say

> the Australian *cooey*, the sound that the simple savages of Australia[13] pitched on to communicate with each other from long distances, is found to be the one which, of all others, travels best over long distances between telephone and telephone. What a jump to make in a few years in this country of ours! *Then*, some perfectly uncivilised natives co-oeing to each other in the forest; now, over the same ground, men of high civilisation *uttering the same sound*[14] from city to city, through one of the most wonderful inventions of modern or of any times.[15]

So long as the telephone could send speech in one direction only, people's minds were held off the idea of conversation. Somewhat ironically, this ensured instead that the instrument would anticipate broadcasting by nearly half a century. Bell himself at first demonstrated his telephone to audiences by playing hymns, recitations, popular songs and attempted to transmit music (not exactly hi-fi quality!), drama and news.[16] Later, opera singers, brass bands, weather reports, time announcements, newspaper dispatches, etc. were added. 'Broadcasting' really started in 1876![17]

It should be remembered that in 1876, the public in the USA were dominated in their thinking about electric communication by the older telegraph. For some time people confused telegraphy with the new 'telephony' and did not grasp the great significance of this new invention.[18] But there was one other, and most important reason, why the enormous social value of the telephone was not immediately realised, which is this: even when Bell succeeded in demonstrating a two-way telephone, so that conversation was possible, this merely connected one person with some other, or one office with another, or one home with another; it was the introduction of the telephone *exchange* that led to the dramatic growth of the telephone as a

system (the idea was simply borrowed from the well-known telegraph exchange of that day). I have elsewhere given my opinion
that, rather than celebrate the centenary of the invention of the
telephone instrument in 1976, as we did,[19] we should have waited
a year or two and celebrated the introduction of the telephone
exchange instead.[20] For it was the coming of the exchange that first
offered people *choice* as to whom they might communicate with; not
only that, but also choice as to where they themselves might wish to
be when phoning others. It is the telephone exchange that endows
the telephone with profound social value, for several reasons which
the business world was very quick to realise.

The first reason is that, with exchanges, the telephone operates in
a *system*, a network, covering the inhabited areas of a country and
today the whole industrialised world and beyond. The global network today is the largest single, interconnected 'machine' in the
world. It is also by far the most complicated.[21] As a network it
enables people for the first time in history to move about the country
and yet appear to stand still (don't we often answer a telephone call
by saying: 'Hello — *where* are you?). A person may leave his office
or home and move about the country (or even abroad today), yet
remain in contact with his home base. Security has thereby been
added to mobility.[22] People now whizz about the world on their
business with complete nonchalance as though it were their natural
right; it has not always been so. Whole new forms of social organisation, habits and customs have been made possible which no longer
require a person to remain located at a fixed point.

It seems wholly natural to us today that colleagues may leave the
office and yet may continue business as though they were still there;
or that industrial units may be located in widely scattered centres,
yet operate in concert; or that government departments need not be
located in the metropolis; or that our children and friends may go on
foreign holidays, yet not appear to us to have vanished into outer
space. Emigration of our relatives has been made just that much
more bearable.

Not only has the telephone service added immeasurably to our
freedom and security of movement, but radio, although unilateral,
has done so too in certain other ways. One of the early results of
radio, in fact, soon after Marconi's pioneering experiments, was a
realisation that naval warfare would be transformed, because ships
could afford to disperse out of sight of one another. Again, with
your pocket transistor you can today travel about the country yet

still receive news bulletins and weather forecasts, hear familiar voices, attend that missed concert *in absentia* — and feel less torn out of your familiar environment than otherwise.

A second reason for the profound social importance of the telephone system is that it is both available to the common man and operable by him for, unlike the telegraph, it requires virtually no skill or training or privilege of ownership.

The introduction of telephone exchanges, which offered people the choice of partner on demand, required some kind of *subscriber organisation*, a kind of club which anyone could join, without qualifications other than the ability to pay. The subscribers not only had rights of usage, but felt that they had. Telephone directories appeared, and any of those listed could assume the right to reach any of the others by virtue of their 'membership'. We are so accustomed to such ideas today that we may forget that such liberties of approach by one person to another, irrespective of rank, did not exist in such egalitarian forms in the nineteenth century. Letters of introduction might have been needed, for example. The telephone service, at one stroke, introduced this totally new concept — that persons of all ranks could be members of the same subscriber organisation, with common rights, rights of 'membership'.

Our thesis then is that the explosive expansion of the telephone service, nationally and internationally, has favoured democratic social relations, and is increasingly doing so as time passes. This is in strict contrast to the social effects of broadcasting, which is essentially a unilateral system, sending out its messages, its information, its instructions, its advertisements, its educational material, etc. from an authoritative centre to the multitude, who cannot effectively respond as *individuals*; broadcasting has enormous responsibilities for this very reason, that it essentially extends and enhances the power of authority. These points will be discussed further in Secion 7.[23]

It is true to say that telephone subscribers' 'rights of membership' were first taken up in the economic or business sphere. There the telephone service was quickly seen to be what it is — a wealth *creating* tool, by virtue of its great assistance to people's organising powers — whereas in the domestic sphere, that is, in homes where income is usually fixed, it was a wealth *consumer*, and is still so today;[24] it is then not surprising to find that the domestic usage of telephones steadily increases as a country's GNP increases whilst the number of telephones per 100 population is roughly constant in the economic sphere in all industrial countries.[25]

Enough about telephones. Let us now turn to a second example of major 'information technology', namely computers, and note again how their actual historical development has differed considerably from early predictions.

The word 'computer' today refers to a very wide range of machines, from the largest multi-million dollar, multi-access machine, to be found in computing centres, to small pocket calculators that you can buy in the shops for a few pounds, which may be used by school-children in class, or for checking bank statements and other domestic chores.

The public imagination was first caught by reports in the popular press in the 1950s about 'electronic brains' — a term which referred to the new automatic, stored-program computers which were beginning to appear in the USA, in Britain and in Germany.[26] These large machines were true innovations and not merely improvements upon existing machines. Prior to these, during World War II, there had been urgent need for certain special purpose, large-scale, computing machines, about which the public then knew nothing owing to legislation on secrecy, including the one called COLOSSUS, situated at Bletchley Park in the UK, which was used in wartime for cryptanalysis.[27] It was this machine that gave stimulus to the building of post-war machines. Another very large special-purpose computer was called ENIAC, which came into service in 1945 for the US Army Ordnance Department and was used for ballistics calculations.[28] The first *general purpose* machines were introduced after World War II, and it was these that may be regarded as conceptually new, and which excited the public with their remarkable powers (both real and imaginary), leading to the myths about 'electronic brains.'[29,30] Such machines were true inventions, which introduced quite new concepts; nothing previously had anticipated them in practical reality.[31] Their conceptual novelty lay in their control by pre-prepared 'programs', written and fed into the machines by their human programmers. These early machines were very expensive, and their use was confined largely to scientific research centres, remote from the general public. Many people then believed that the world's needs would be satisfied by a few such machines and 'No-one in the world foresaw the boom which has made the industry grow so explosively since about 1960'.[32] One of the early difficulties facing those who were trying to per-suade business and industry to take an interest in these new machines was that programming had yet to be developed that was reliable and straightforward and that could be used by people other than mathematicians. Lord Bowden of Chesterfield has spoken of his own experiences when trying to sell these machines to industries in North America:

> I had to sell the wretched things, if I was to earn my living and keep my firm in business. I decided that I had the most peculiar job in the world, until I met a man on the [steamship] Queen Mary who sold lighthouses on commission and he told me about some of his problems![32]

As time passed machines became even larger in size, faster in operation, and with ever greater capacities for storing data (in their so-called 'memories'). The computer business came to develop a 'life of its own' with its designers and users, which sometimes took on some semblance to a cult, with its own private jargon, its exclusiveness and mystique.

For some years it appeared that the future of these machines resided in our ability to increase their size, their capital cost and power, so it seemed that they would increasingly retreat into scientific research laboratories or into special centres from which their services could be rented out to research workers. To the general public they became increasingly remote and shrouded in mystery. However, their history proved to be quite otherwise, for in recent years the computer industry has expanded into a totally new market — for small pocket computers for use by the public — much to the surprise of many.

It should be remembered that 'simple' desk-type calculators had already existed since the seventeenth century — Pascal built a mechanical adding machine in 1642, and Leibnitz a multiplying machine in 1694. It was these machines which were the ancestors of many kinds of desk machine that were not at all unfamiliar to many members of the public; every shop-assistant could use a cash-register without feelings of mystique, and many office workers already used desk calculators of all sorts; most older children could use a slide-rule. It is such things as these that were already familiar to the public in the 1950s when reports of the new 'giant brains' sprang upon them.

The computer industry began to produce programmed machines that were smaller in scale and which were not beyond the purses of business and industry, and which could be operated by persons of less training. In addition the computer industry began to develop the *multi-access* idea, by which a single very large scale, expensive machine could be called upon to supply computing services to many users simultaneously, in various geographical locations, in a manner somewhat analogous to that in which the services of a telephone exchange were effectively rented by the telephone subscribers. For example, the I.P. Sharp Associates system operates over leased lines between North America, Europe and Australia, with centralised computers located in Toronto. Several hundred users have access to the system simultaneously, either through their own terminals or by using Telex machines, thereby loading the computers more uniformly round the clock. Such a system also provides access to 'data bases', giving customers extensive information about economic, demographic, banking, actuarial, industrial and other matters, such as the Prestel system may do too, on a grand scale, for the general public.[33]

It appeared that the early expectations about the future of programmed computers had, not unreasonably, failed to predict the dramatic changes in electronic techniques and manufacture, that were to come about in the 1960s and 70s, nor had they adequately reckoned with the insight of certain professional classes, other than scientists. First, certain major industries, together with banking, insurance and other financial institutions, found that they could beneficially use the services of modern programmed computers, either by buying one of modest size or by renting the usage of a large-scale machine. These industries too handled numerical data in great quantities, and their needs were not wholly dissimilar to those of the science research laboratory.

Computers came to create a market in accountancy; banks, financial houses, commerce and industry provided outlets for their use, and soon the general public began to find its bank statements appearing in new and rather strange forms (not always helpful, in my opinion) and its accounts becoming 'computerised' etc. The public began to form a new image of what computers were, for they had now entered people's lives directly.

Other professionals eventually came to see that computers could be of great value to them, in particular those who were concerned with industrial design and other design problems. *Experiments* in design could be made and the results tested, without expenditure of labour, time, money and materials on actual construction of prototypes.

It would be tedious to continue with further examples. As the reader will know, the image of computers and their powers became steadily transformed in the public mind.[34] The market for computers widened greatly, and research was applied to finding electronic techniques that would cheapen their usage and consequently expand the market further — to cover not only industry, the professions, banking, insurance (the economic sphere), but the common man himself and the housewife. To achieve this aim the technology had to take an about-turn, and become ever cheaper, smaller and simpler to use. Children today do not use log tables and slide-rules — they have their own pocket calculators.

The cheapness and widespread use of the pocket machines is a modern phenomenon; they are usable by almost anybody, without training, at least for their commonest tasks, and have become familiar, domestic things. Few people understand their workings, nor do they need to. They are 'foolproof'. Most important of all, they are an example of a technology which can help to free the general public just a little from the grip of the professional 'expert'. The essential power which they offer to the lay person is an enormous magnification of what limited ability he may have to carry out complex rational operations. The individual is thereby more able to arm himself against those institutions (professional, commercial, governmental, etc.) which threaten him by virtue of their organised 'bureaucratic' powers for dealing with very complex 'rational' matters, e.g. the income tax inspector, the VAT man, banks, etc.

Other technologies have appeared recently which also serve to protect the lay individual or to guide him through the complex world of business, trade, law, finance, news and all the other elements of today's 'rational' organisations; and his pocket computer may go with him as he does so. For example, in Britain we have the new Prestel service of the Post Office, which may be used without any special skills.[35] This service provides information to the user, both in his home and at the office, which he asks for by pressing numbered buttons, according to code numbers denoting the items of interest, which are listed in his special directory. At home he might ask for help over holiday accommodation, or theatres and cinemas, on gardening, football results — or even help with taxation and legal matters. In the office he might require information from government departments, banks, the Stock Exchange, insurance companies, transport and exporting agencies, etc. Furthermore, the user may himself send data into the computer and operate with the system inter-actively. A host of varied institutions provide the necessary information, updated regularly by telephoning the computer — e.g. government departments, industry and trade, the Stock Exchange, libraries, travel agents, the press, etc. It is possible that we may soon see Prestel used by the common man for helping him complete his income tax forms or for checking the accuracy of tax demands, aided by using his pocket calculator!

These cheap pocket calculators, being very portable, also offer their users various facilities whilst they are travelling about. Their appearance has created a totally new class of market, quite unforseen when computers first appeared in the 1950s. Of course, the development of large, multi-access, programmed computers has continued, and these too offer freedom of movement to their professional users in the same way that the telephone network offers us all greater freedom of movement — that is, because they are connected to large networks, operating both nationally and internationally. These large computers are expensive and immobile, but they do not need to centralise their powers for that reason as was at first often imagined would be the case. Their operations are highly dispersed, and switchable on demand from remote points in a way analogous to those of telephone exchanges. They support the trend towards dispersal of large industries today for the same reasons.

As argued before, telecommunication and computer networks may serve to support either centralisation or decentralisation of power. They offer us the choice, and our decision is political.[36] They can assist centralisation by enabling a central authority to obtain information from, and to direct the activities of dispersed units or, on the contrary, they may encourage decentralisation by offering the various organs of industry, business, government, etc. the liberty of dispersal, with the choice of operating in concert. The increasing tendency today is towards decentralisation, which is possible only with our modern communication networks (telephone, Telex, computer, etc.), and our familiarity with these encourages our thoughts in that direction. But this does not imply that 'telecommunication is replacing travel' by obviating the need to commute from home to a central place of work; we shall be arguing to the contrary in Section 8 of this chapter.

3. The 'Chip': Technology and Crisis[37]

The expression 'the chip'[38] strikes fear into many breasts today. Again, it is an outcome that was totally unforseen in earlier days of computers, for the technology that has led to its creation — microelectronics — did not exist, and was unthinkable. The 'chip' is the supreme example of 'information technology', for such devices show no apparent limit to their increasing scale and powers to process recorded information and data. They raise glaring question marks over some of our older, traditional industries.

Whereas, in the early nineteenth century it was the labouring classes who feared and reacted to the introduction of new machinery, with good cause, it is the highly skilled and even certain professional sections today who feel most threatened by 'the chip'. The Luddites [39] smashed the machinery of their masters in their despair — the modern skilled worker may simply refuse to operate it and strike, with rather similar feelings. These fears have appeared prominently today in the newspaper industry, especially in Britain where the industry is still largely a traditional craft industry, and where Fleet Street has continued to cling to the old-fashioned linotype method of printing and seems to be fearful of facing the consequences of computerised production. It is a political hot potato, which has been grasped more quickly in North America, but very slowly indeed in Britain and Europe.

The main economic problem is raised by the fact that a few hundred pounds today will buy the computing power which cost ten million pounds in the 1950s, when computers first came onto the scene, whilst the people themselves, skilled in their craft, are becoming ever more expensive. Not surprisingly, this problem is frequently interpreted politically (though quite falsely) as 'technology *versus* people'. It is an emotional judgement made under strong feelings of threat, but false because technology has no power in itself; it cannot be blamed or commended, only people may be.[40] As one British trade unionist has put it: 'To look at microelectronics in terms of job losses is like viewing the invention of the wheel in terms of an increase in road accidents'.

Similar causes of anxiety are appearing today in many other spheres of economic life besides the newspaper industry, and many are the predictions that are made about the transformations which may occur in our industrial societies during the twenty years that are left of this millenium. Many writers have offered the view that we are now at a turning point — and they well may be right. Many have made their predictions, and only time will show. It is, after all, less than thirty years since we first spoke in a self-conscious manner of 'development' of the ex-colonial countries, few of which had yet become independent nations,[41] whilst today we realise that every action that we take in the industrial countries is now intently and critically watched by these same peoples. In that same short time there has grown a widespread concern with human values other than economic growth, and increasing feeling that our political objectives ought to be more concerned with quality of life.[42] Economic criteria are no longer adequate;[43] in Schumacher's phrase they must be reconsidered 'as if people mattered'.[44] Examination and criticism of capitalism itself has exercised many minds for over a century, but no comparable weight of thought has yet been applied to the industrial system with its goals, its social values, its relationship to the state, or with how it may transform itself in the future; as John Galbraith has remarked, the industrial system seems to have created a widespread belief that it has reached finality: 'one does not wonder where one is going if one is already there'.[45]

Although it is no substitute for thought or for the creation of new objectives, the feeling that we have reached a turning point is certainly abroad in the land, and the present hullabaloo about the 'chip' is merely symptomatic of this. What awaits us around the corner is pure speculation, 'futurology', which may certainly express people's changed ideals or fears but which cannot represent reliable prediction. As Dennis Gabor has so rightly said, you can only *invent* the future. The vast powers that the 'technology of information' has now to offer us, in both its computer and its telecommunication modes, represent only a great change in the conditions that now bear upon the planning and operation of our economic, political and other social institutions. These technological powers themselves cannot decide how we shall come to adjust our behaviour nor our policies, nor our details, so as to adapt to these rapidly changing conditions; that is a matter of political wisdom, for there may be many alternatives. We shall not make it our business how to gaze into the crystal ball, but will leave this to others with greater insight and imagination.[46]

4. The Power of Technology Lies in its Possession

Technology has no power in itself to take overt action; only people have; it is not open to blame or praise; so how can it be that it so often arouses strong feelings? The Luddites smashed the weaving frames; the first railway engines were feared as inventions of the Devil, as they spouted sparks and flames; television has been denounced as the destroyer of our children. So wherein does the power of technology lie?

It has been said that the power of technology lies in the hands of those who use it. However, it may exert power without actually being used, in any overt sense. The most glaring example today is the atomic bomb, for it is enough merely to possess it, without necessarily using it; the present day balance of terror is achieved through its existence and its possession by certain states. The same is literally true of other technologies — their power lies in their possession and the *possibility* of their usage, by individuals or by groups.

The power of technology, through the forms of its possession by individuals or by organisations, operates in two ways. First, it offers its possessors power over both the environment and over other people; weapons, tools, industrial machinery, household equipment, personal belongings — all offer the possessor certain overt powers of *action*. Secondly, and more subtly, technology exerts power over its possessors themselves, existentially; the mere fact that you own an automobile, or a box of tools, or a house full of furniture and equipment, makes you care for them in certain ways. You may even love your automobile; you may be deeply hurt if your house is burgled (even though well insured) and feel it is an assault on yourself; again, you may feel compelled to use the things which you own, simply because you have bought them. In such ways possessions make slaves of us all, whilst they may liberate us in so doing.

Our possession of technical artefacts sets both forms of power into action — overt and existential. Possession is then not a passive thing, but is essentially *activity*;[47] an artefact is always possessed *as* something. For example, you may own a typewriter, but it is only a typewriter if used as such, whereas, if you are unable to type, it becomes an ornament, a piece of sculpture, a relic, an embarrassment to be sold as soon as possible, or merely a status symbol. In every case it is essentially *acting as* something, in your possession. Secondly, it acts upon you, as its possessor, *demanding* your attention, making you feel that you ought to write that letter, or simply *offering* you pride of possession — always active. The particular artefacts which you possess have symbolic values; they tell other people much about yourself, whilst you in turn feel that they both express and satisfy your personal interests and tastes.

The word 'possession' is very ambiguous, for there are many forms which it may take, in various legal or political guises; these various forms and styles of possession greatly influence the nature and extent of the powers which the technology proffers. It may be possessed outright by an individual and under his unquestioned control, or by a corporation; machines and equipment may be held under license from others; or they may be owned co-operatively, by a group; or they may be public property; or they may be rented, etc.

The nature and extent of the power that technology offers to industry or to others who possess it (and also of its power over them) depends upon people's abilities to use it, and this does not neces-sarily mean the individual's skills or intelligences but also their forms of social organisation, e.g. their types of industrial structures, the efficiency and integrity of their 'bureaucratic' superstructures, their arrangements for raw-material supplies, their control over component manufacturers, etc. Thus, the power of, say, a major automobile company to execute its plans may be frustrated by a labour strike in some ancillary plant — just as surely as the benefits of some technical aid programme, intended to serve some poor developing country, may sometimes become frustrated if the neces-sary political, educational or industrial organisations are not adequately set up to support it,[48] perhaps leaving the plant and equipment to be seized by some existing elite for their own prestige purposes. Technology is a political matter, not only within indus-trial nations but within the developing world too.

As was argued in Chapter 1, technological 'progress' and indus-trialisation do not come to a society as a free gift, but they always exact some social price.[49] Although the majority of new machines and equipment that appear on the market are no more than improvements over existing things, which is not particularly socially disturbing, there have been certain rare moments in history when some radically new invention, or discovery suddenly offers society completely new possibilities, conceptually new modes of action, new alternatives, to which it must eventually adjust. The invention of the wheel, or the discovery of new uses of fire are sometimes referred to as examples, but we might equally well refer to the spinning jenny, or the first railways, or the telephone, or radio, television, computers, the 'chip' — the pace has accelerated, and today the spate of radical invention in the field of electronics has become a torrent.

What has been invented cannot be un-invented. It may perhaps be resisted by some, but it is there, in the mind if not in the metal. Society must adapt and change itself and its institutions. New ones are created, old ones die, and some people may not wholly like the changes. There are two opposing ways of responding to this situation of ceaseless change resulting from the need to adapt to the torrent of modern technology; one way is to go 'back to the land', to 'opt out'; but such a reactionary, emotional response is self-defeating, simply because the powers of action offered by the technology will not be obliterated from the minds of these new-style peasants. The other response is to judge the technology rationally and to decide what benefits it may possibly offer; not to accept it blindly, or aim to be in fashion, but to be critical and to decide upon alternative policies and to make one's choice. In either case, the new technology cannot be wholly ignored; it is a fact.

5. Technology Regarded as 'Liberties of Action'

In Section 4, and elsewhere in the book, emphasis has been placed upon regarding technology as an *activity*, [50] rather than as material artefacts (machines, instruments, tools). A specific artefact offers certain powers of action to its user and, in turn, it acts upon the user, his feelings, attitudes and thoughts. Further, that activity is always carried out within some social context.

The various uses to which a particular artefact may be applied may be numerous, and the future may find further totally new uses for it; they will essentially depend upon the social context (how people live, their work and leisure activities, the economic and other social conditions) together with the physical environment (urban or rural, the weather, the geography, raw materials). Whatever these uses may turn out to be, they can only employ the basic 'liberties of action' which the artefact offers and, equally important, they will be constrained by the law, morals, customs and economics of the society. Technology *permits*, but the law *forbids*..

Let us illustrate with an example: the telephone service. What basic 'liberties of action' does this offer? (We have already partly examined the question in Section 2).

A telephone system is an interconnected network of exchanges, covering a wide geographical area, such that one telephone at one point A may be connected to *any* other telephone, at another point B, for the purposes of conversation, under the choice of the person at point A. Now it may be thought that this is the whole story — but it is not so. The important thing about the telephone service is that two people conversing need not be at fixed points A and B but they might be *anywhere* in the network. For example, suppose we call the two people Mr Smith and Mr Brown; then Mr Smith may stay at his office whilst Mr Brown moves about the country knowing that he is able to ring Mr Smith from any point in the network as he does so. Furthermore, if he leaves an advance telephone number with Mr Smith, that gentleman may ring him back if he so desires. It is not necessary to know *where* your partner is situated when telephoning; geography is replaced by a number-code system which requires no training to use.

In other words, the basic 'liberty of action' that the telephone service offers us is the freedom to move about whilst remaining in social contact.[51] The partners may be mobile yet appear to each other to be stationary. The introduction of the telephone service, 100 years ago, bought great freedom of movement to people, whilst adding to their security to a degree that is difficult for us to imagine today.[52]

Or consider another example: the railway network. To be brief, this enables goods, persons and written messages (e.g. mail) to be transported with great security, between selected places, according to pre-arranged time schedules that are necessitated by the fact that trains must stay on the lines (on which they cannot overtake), that they can be only at one place at any time, that they are finite in number, together with other physical constraints. They also require operating staff who, not unreasonably, introduce their own rules.

These simple examples merely illustrate the idea of physical 'liberties of action' which the technologies make *conceivably* possible. But, in practice, there are various constraints, legal, economic, moral, customary, etc., which bear upon what people actually do with these liberties, when they put the technologies into use.

Consequently, the practical usages of a piece of equipment, or a technical system, together with the values that result, are likely to vary considerably in different countries, according to their social conditions, their histories, and their traditions. The 'liberties of action' offered by the technology can do no more than encourage or guide people's thoughts and activities in certain general directions, but no more.[53] The people of a society which possesses computers, aircraft, atomic power stations and other 'high' technology may act, think and feel very differently from those of another that possesses only bows and arrows and cooking pots. But these possessions alone do not decide exactly what their social differences shall be, nor how they will develop.

6. On Technical 'Liberties of Action' and 'Social Action'

What we have called the 'liberties of action' offered by a particular technological system are simply the elementary actions that it renders conceivably possible, whereas the *usages* of that system refer to the practical operations that a people carries out within its particular context. In order to clarify this complex subject we may perhaps take a lead from Max Weber's analysis of political action.[54]

Weber divided all human action into two classes, one being 'social action', and it is that that concerns us here because, in this book, we are considering the technology of communication in particular; and communication is always a social activity. By 'social action' Weber meant all human behaviour to which the actor attaches a subjective meaning; further, the action is social only inasmuch as it takes account of, and is directed towards other people's behaviour. This view of 'social action' is very much in line with the ideas of the pragmatists in their treatment of the theory of meaning.[55] Suffice it to interpret this here by saying that communication proceeds by 'sign-behaviour'; a 'sign' is any human behaviour to which significance (a 'meaning') is attributed both by the actor and the recipient — a shared social activity. For example, during a conversation a remark made by one of the partners is intended by him to affect the other in some way, in particular to elicit a relevant reply from him. At the same time the partner may be making many other actions which are neither intended to be meaningful nor are they interpreted as meaningful; these are not 'sign-behaviour', neither are they 'social actions'.

It is the purpose of the technology of communication and of information to extend our human powers of 'sign-behaviour', which is essentially 'social action' and, as argued before, this technology can be seen to have a specific value or significance only within some specific social context.[56] Max Weber expressed the view generally by saying that we can *understand* something (e.g. some machine) only through the significance which it may have for human action, both in its production and its usage.[57]

The specific values and significance which some technological artefact, or system, holds for a particular society will be revealed by the people's activities. It may be a computer, say, or a modern telephone system, or a printing press; what is important is what people actually *do* with it and what changes occur in their other activities as a result of their possessing it. Thus, they may perhaps use it to help them reorganise their industrial production, or to improve their transport facilities, or to promote education or entertainment; again, they may use it for propaganda purposes or merely for window-dressing, prestige, purposes; or it may come into public use and create new social habits and customs as, say, railways did last century, or as television has done in modern times. The activities may be industrial, cultural, military, political, scientiric, educational — the same technology may mean very different things to different people.

Max Weber argued that all human action has components which fall into 3 distinct classes:

(1a) rational action towards a goal;
(1b) rational action towards a value;
(2)   emotional action;
(3)   traditional (habitual) action.

Rational action towards a goal is action according to rules, laws, scientific or logical principles, in order to achieve some specific end or 'goal'.[58] For example, as when doing a calculation or when designing a piece of machinery, or when a solicitor advises a client on some legal matter. Rational action towards a value means acting in some deliberate, intended way simply because the desired outcome is worthwhile or is valued in some way; for example, as when going to attend a concert or when going to visit a sick friend. Both these classes of action are *rational*, one being directed to some external goal and the other to an internal goal of satisfaction or morality.[59]

Emotional action is action, without reason, expressing one's feelings, impulses, desires or hates, etc. as when cheering in the crowd at a football match, or when crying your eyes out at a cinema; no intention or purpose is implied.

Traditional action means habitual or customary action, as when standing for the national anthem, or when lapsing into clichés in conversation, or always walking to the office by the same route, etc.

This classification does not imply that any one of our complex actions is wholly rational, or emotional or habitual; it may contain elements of all three.

For example, consider a telephone conversation. It may be that one person is telephoning another for some deliberate purpose, perhaps to arrange a meeting — as a rational, goal-directed action. So he frames his words and phrases with due deliberation, with that goal in view. At the same time he may also feel that a call to his old friend was long overdue, so he is also phoning with that objective in view; that too is a rational action. But at the same time much of his speech consists of emotional elements, interjections, laughs, stressings, etc., which help to express his feelings — emotional actions. Furthermore, his speech closely conforms to the rules of spoken language, whilst many of his remarks are made by sheer habit. Whatever complex pattern of human action is considered, it may be regarded at these three categorically distinct levels — the rational, the emotional and the traditional (habitual).

Let us return to our earlier point and consider the values and purposes of a particular technology to societies with different social conditions. As argued before, the technology merely offers certain elemental 'liberties of action' to the users; the uses to which people put their enhanced power are (following Weber) describable in terms of the three levels of human action — the rational, emotional and traditional levels. We may now ask: Why should it be that different peoples use similar technologies in such widely varying ways? Max Weber would almost certainly have argued against technological determinism, the idea that the technology decides what precise uses it shall be put to. What then guides different people's usages into different directions? Clearly it is the result of their social differences — cultural, economic, political, educational, demographic, etc., together with their different physical environments, including all their other technologies. It is this host of forces that shapes our human values and desires which govern our actions.

Weber spoke of *domination*[60] in reference to the complex and varied social pressures and constraints which bear upon a people, shaping their desires, their motives, their allegiances, their acceptance of law and authority and their obedience to government, etc; his aim was to build a science of social action.[61] He was essentially concerned with political and economic action, whereas here we are using his concepts in a somewhat different context in order to understand better how people's actions and attitudes are mediated by their possession of technology, especially the 'technology of information'. Weber argued that these forces, which dominate people's thoughts, feelings and so actions, fall into three distinct classes:

(1)   rational domination;
(2)   charismatic domination;
(3)   traditional domination.

where (1) refers to the forces exerted by law, decrees, and regulations, to which we could add logic and scientific laws, whilst (2) refers to the influence of great leaders, or heroes and people of outstandng example (from religious figures to successful business magnates); and (3) refers to engrained habits, customs and perhaps including moral codes. In practice, elements of all these may be needed when examining our complex social behaviour; they are simply analytic concepts.

In summary, the power which technology appears to have over people, whether those of our modern, so-called [62] affluent 'technological societies' or of tribal groups, does not stem from the technology itself, with its particular 'liberties of action' that it renders possible, any more than a technology itself can decide the uses for which it is most suitable. The power arises from its possession by people who live within some particular social, legal, political, economic, framework which decides the mode of that possession (i.e. the conditions under which the people possess it, their rights of possession and usage, their traditions and education, their economic status, etc.) and which controls them rationally, charismatically, and traditionally.

It was Max Weber's contention that our modern industrial societies are dominated largely by rationality directed towards goals, as was discussed in Chapter 1. They are characterised by their rational economic activity, through their intense degree of organisation with its highly structured 'bureaucracies', their control by accountancy, their increasing use of science, their hierarchical systems of command within clear systems of law and with stated economic goals.

The dominant technological element of this intense and increasing rationality may be traced back historically to the invention of clocks; the clock has dominated our behaviour for a long time in industrial society, with its time schedules, planned sequencing of operations and daily routines of work. To quote Lewis Mumford: 'the clock, not the steam engine, is the key machine of the modern industrial age'.[63] And the clock is an *information* (organising) technology, not a power (production) technology. Its dominance was enhanced last century by factory regulations and the 'moving belt' production line and further still later by the coming of radio, with its programmes emitted to a time schedule over whole countries simultaneously to millions of people. The computer has come more recently to enhance further the rational domination of industrial societies.

Now it will be noticed that Max Weber's three classes of domination over our actions do not correspond precisely with his four classes of possible action, listed earlier. Raymond Aron, commenting upon the point, observes that Weber himself was not consistent in his writings and sometimes used other classifications.[64] However, the *rational* classes of action and of domination do correspond; rational action towards either a goal or a value is rational in either case. Again, *emotional action* and *charismatic domination* both suggest psychological motivation. Aron suggests that the three basic human motivations are essentially *reason, emotion* and *sentiment*, and that these are to be regarded as purely analytic concepts.

It may well be argued that these three are never independent. For example, our reasoning is governed by habit (tradition); we *conform* to the rule of law, rather than *obey* it because most of us do not know the law in detail; again we conform to the rules of arithmetic, or to the syntax of our language, without expressly thinking about the rules as we do so. Rational action towards a value is especially governed by tradition, of one's culture and religious background. Our actions are continually governed by habit, as Hume observed. Again, to be rational we must desire to be so; emotion must precede reason. They are inseparable, although the contrary is not true, for we can neither be reasoned into a mood nor out of it. Nevertheless, the three classes (reason, emotion and sentiment) still remain as analytic concepts.

To return to our original theme of technology and its values to people of different cultures and conditions, where we have been regarding technology as *activity* rather than as artefacts-in-the-metal. It is convenient and helpful to keep those three classes of motivation in mind when involved in the complexities of argument about such topical matters as, for example, technological aid for developing countries, and whether these countries need modern equipment or only 'intermediate technology', or why the equipment is sometimes not put to use; or, similarly, when considering the technological 'progress' of the affluent countries and what it means; or about people's real motives for buying the latest domestic machines and gadgets (technological *fashion*); or even about workers' fearing the introduction of new technology into their traditional industries, etc. The acquisition, usage and appreciation of a new machine or system is not wholly a rational matter, not only in pre-industrial countries but in the modern industrial world too, however much we pride ourselves that we purchase it for sound economic reasons. At the crudest level, one only has to think of some of our office equipment and machinery (which may be acquired for reasons of fashion or prestige) — or the purchase of that latest model of automobile. . .

Let us next examine and compare two examples of modern technology in this spirit — broadcasting and the telephone service. It is only too commonly that these are lumped together and called 'communication systems', whereas they are sharply to be contrasted, not only at the rational level, but at the levels of emotion and sentiment as well.

7. Unilateral versus Bilateral 'Communication' Services; Their Vital Social Distinctions and Values

The word 'communication' is today becoming a grossly overworked word.[65] One common source of confusion is failure to make any distinction between the unilateral services (e.g. radio and television broadcasting,[66] newspapers etc.) and the bilateral services (e.g. the telephone service, postal service, telegraphs, etc.). Let us look at this distinction in the spirit of Section 6; i.e. their social functions in terms of the 'liberties of action' which they offer. It will be argued that the various *unilateral* services are, strictly speaking, not communication services at all, but that they are more correctly to be called *dissemination* (or, simply, *broadcast* systems), for they do not permit individual people to answer back. One's feelings are totally different when telephoning, even a stranger, from when listening to the radio.

The various bilateral services (telephone, post etc.) which permit people to share in conversation, either spoken or written, (and sometimes with other forms of sign-usage) may be considered as technical extensions of our natural powers of speech and language — powers which we learn from birth, with extraordinary speed, first with our mothers and continued throughout life with every social encounter. Conversation continually re-socialises us, brings us into the world. Conversation, together with all our gestures and body-signs,[67] is the vital human, social, process of *sharing* (i.e. communication): it is the essential social activity that brings each of us into our particular world and which simultaneously gives each of us our sense of individual existence as a person.[68,69]

During conversation one person makes a remark and the other responds, either by replying or by making some other significant action, thereby giving *interpretation* to the first remark. The two have then *shared*. This elemental social act, remark and reply, is one of our most common social experiences, so familiar to us that we may seldom give attention to the miracle, which is what it truly is.[70] The telephone and other bilateral services, which operate in the conversational, inter-active mode, extend these natural powers of language, spoken or written — they enable replies to be made to remarks, thereby giving interpretation, an essentially social act. Even though one person is a dominating bully and the other is frightened into silence, that relationship is revealed to both of them; they are nevertheless still communicating.

By contrast, unilateral services such as radio broadcasting, are 'almost against nature'. The thousands of individual listeners may each be reacting in their own ways — some agreeing with the speaker, some bored, some angered — but their thousands of interpretations are not directly revealed to the broadcaster. There is no social, reciprocal, interpretative act of sharing taking place. Anyone who has ever made a broadcast talk knows how strange it feels, sitting in the studio talking not to another person but to a thing (a microphone) which doesn't reply; one has neither knowledge nor feeling about any individual listener's existence (perhaps nobody is listening?). Our relation to a thing differs from our relation to a person.[71] It is for this reason that doubt may be cast upon the word 'communication' in connection with radio, television, books, newspapers, and all the unilateral services. They will be referred to in this book as *broadcasting services* or as *disseminating services*, in order to distinguish them.

To be fair, any responsible broadcasting authority will pay great attention to the public response by carrying out listener and viewer surveys, etc., just as any newspaper will publish a few 'Letters to the Editor'. But the first is 'consensus feedback', not individual responses, whilst the second represents responses from a trivial fraction of the audience or the readership. Again, many devices are adopted by broadcasting authorities to encourage response from individuals, such as 'phone-ins', etc.; yet, even so, it is only to those few who phone-in that the mode appears to be conversational (bilateral) whilst to the thousands of others listening or watching these few are themselves heard or seen as performers.[72] The motivations of the two groups will differ. Nothing can be done to convert a broadcast programme into a public meeting of listeners or viewers.

All broadcasting services must therefore be authoritarian in some way and to some extent or other, because they are unilateral. Not only for this reason but also because they are forced to be selective; e.g. they must choose how to use their limited hours and select their performers. As a result they are laid wide open to public comment, criticism and often concern — such is inescapable. Being unilateral, they serve to enhance social conformities of certain kinds — new fashions, new habits, sayings, customs, heroes, aspirations — but all societies owe their existences to conformities, whether desirable, or not. Broadcasting, being unilateral, will be seen by some as 'teacher', or as the voice of government, or of 'big business', or of 'our Leader' — as *them* in some sense or other; it must always appear to be authoritarian, for this is inherent in the nature of broadcasting. Broadcasting policy must then be expected to vary among different countries very much according to each country's conditions and its people's political wisdom, for it dominates them not only rationally, but charismatically above all. It is the modern oracle. The way of broadcasting is hard and its responsibilities are immense, a fact that was recognised from the beginning.[73] However, radio, television, the press, and all unilateral systems of 'broadcasting' involve not one, but two kinds of authority. First, there is the administration, the body which controls, plans, operates and generally makes the system possible, and secondly, the authority of the performers themselves — the selected speakers, actors, announcers, playwrights, etc. It is only the latter whom the public sees and hears and forms many opinions about; it is they who may be seen as 'stars', who may exert charisma, who may set fashions and styles of speech, who select topics for attention, and who may encourage or discourage trends in musical taste; and it is largely through their satisfaction or dissatisfaction with these performers that the public senses the reputation of the administration authority behind them.

The relationship between these two authorities, the administration and the performers, is very complex, and far from being understood. Inasmuch as all unilateral ('broadcasting') services must rouse problems of monopoly (both of administration and of performers) they are highly political affairs, inevitably raising questions of 'the right to broadcast', 'political bias', 'selection of news', 'people's right to know', etc. They are all faced with problems of developing *trust*, with no universal solution because they operate within varied socio/political/religious value-systems. They cannot keep all the people happy all the time.

On the contrary, the bilateral services such as the telephone, the post,[74] inter-active computer-links, etc. require only one authority — that for administration. In nearly all countries of the world this authority comes either directly from the government (e.g. the various PTTs) or indirectly by license or by contract, for they are vital to the national economy and to security.[75]

These bilateral services, too, do not escape public criticism (e.g. the telephone service), but now, distinct from television or radio, the public are themselves the 'performers'. Criticism, when it comes, is then criticism by the 'performers' of the administrative authority. Consequently, we must expect public attitudes to the bilateral services to differ sharply from those to the unilateral services. Without wishing to seem facetious, this difference could be summarised by saying that telephones are criticised when they don't work, whereas television is frequently under criticism when it *does* work!

Again, the contemptuous expression 'mass communication'[76] is applied only to the unilateral services (radio, television, the press, etc.) and never to the bilateral. Curiously, there is one particular unilateral service which escapes this fate — namely, books. Who exactly are 'the masses' except you and me. 'The masses' have no objective existence.[77]

If we are to single out one bilateral service and label it as 'the most indispensible', at least to industrial countries, that one would surely be the telephone service, national and international. To many people the word '*telephone*' may conjure up an image of the thing in the sitting-room at home, that is to say the *domestic sphere* of usage. This instrument may greatly add to one's security at home and to the planning and organising of domestic affairs, but it is in the *economic sphere* that we find our utter dependence upon it, within industrial nations — for trade, industry, commerce, finance, government and all the organised institutions of industrial society.[78] The same may be said of the international telephone service since the end of World War II, not only of its values for new services, business, finance, etc, but essentially for its resulting effects upon international relations, activities, and public attitudes. This service, now of global scale, offers 'liberties of action' which cannot be ignored, and access to it is sought by even the poorest countries.[79] It is hard to believe today that in 1938, the British Prime Minister Neville Chamberlain could have referred to Germany's annexation of the Sudetenland as a 'quarrel in a far-away country between people of whom we know nothing'.

The global telephone network, linking the internal networks of all the continents, is the biggest machine in the world and its usage is increasing 'explosively'. Why should this be? Several answers may be given but, essentially, it is because this bilateral telephone system is by far the most flexible machine there is; it does not produce only one, or a finite range, of products as does manufacturing machinery, but it serves an unlimited variety of human purposes. It has as many functions as has language itself. Some may protest that computers are even more flexible, but this is not so, for they operate with language systems[80] and not with human language. Flexibility of both global and national networks arises also from the fact that they form an interconnected system of *exchanges*, whether they be used for conversation or for data, offering unlimited choice (apart from costs) of social contact between any two of the world's subscribers.[81] The greatest precautions and security methods are employed to ensure reliable operation of the telephone system, in peace, civil disturbance, or war, for its collapse would be catastrophic. We have organised our affairs around our trusting assumption that it is always available, and we cannot well imagine life as it was before its introduction.[82]

Yet the telephone service, *as* a service, is barely 100 years old. Its introduction in the 1870s and its extraordinarily rapid adoption by business and industry, especially in the USA,[83] did not merely signify the coming of a new consumer market; it was a creative act, comparable only to the introduction of the printing press into Europe in the fifteenth century,[84] for it led to a transformation of social attitudes and habits of a most profound kind. Its coming was truly 'revolutionary'. All our more modern systems such as the high-speed telegraph (e.g. Telex), inter-active computer links, data networks, etc. continue traditions which the telephone service started, but they cannot supplant it. There are several reasons for this view, the overwhelming one being that the telephone simply extends all the values of human speech, discussion, conversation, decision-making — over an unlimited geographical area; it requires no skills or training, but only our natural habits of speech. It also enables us to choose our partners (as suggested in Section 2, it is the telephone *exchanges* which give the service such great importance).[85]

Those who subscribe to the telephone not only have certain rights of talking to others, but also feel that they have. It is like a *right of membership*, not a *right of possession*. Messages are not commodities, to be bought or sold, so when you telephone someone in order to make an enquiry you are simply exercising your 'right to know' and not a 'right to have', for you are taking nothing from them. These two kinds of right are fundamentally different; as was stressed in Chapter 1, 'communication' means *sharing* — but essentially sharing by participation, not sharing by division.[86]

However, it is the caller who usually feels such rights most strongly, not always the receiver, for it is he who has made the choice. The receiver may sometimes feel that he *is* being deprived of something by the caller, namely his privacy; in that rather abstract sense the caller is exercising his 'right to possession' (of his partner's privacy). People may therefore feel that their domestic telephone exposes them to unwelcome intrusion, forgetting that this is the inevitable price to be paid for their own right to make calls. Their protection is to apply to the telephone authorities for their number to be withheld from the book; and that may appear to other subscribers as something more than a desire for privacy, even as selfishness or arrogance.[87] For refusal to communicate *is* an act of communication, and often a powerful one.

I have suggested elsewhere that the technology of the telephone service, being bilateral and operable by the public through its system of exchanges, is more favourable to the development of democratic relationships than is broadcasting, which is necessarily centralised, exclusive and authoritarian, thereby seeming to be more favourable to centralised authority. However, this should not be read as an argument for technological determinism, because it is saying nothing whatever about the *natures* of the 'democracies' or 'authoritarian powers' that may be created by different societies. What a people or government actually does with the 'liberties of action' that these two contrasting technologies offer is a matter of their choice, a choice that will depend upon a host of factors — their historical experience and their existing political, educational and other institutions, their degree of development, etc. We cannot fail to notice that the purposes and significances of broadcasting vary enormously among the countries of this world; but what is far less well known is that the adoption and usages of their internal telephone services vary just as much (even taking national wealths into account).[88]

Ithiel de Sola Pool has raised an interesting question in this connection.[89] Why was it that the telephone, originally seen by the public as a 'broadcasting medium' very rapidly dropped this role and became adopted instead wholly for private conversation?[90] Broadcasting had to wait for another half-century before becoming reality (although the concept was there) when the technique of radio was developed, largely by Marconi.[91] Ithiel de Sola Pool has remarked that these facts illustrate a crucial point of difference between the theories of Karl Marx and Max Weber. Marx would perhaps have argued for technological determinism, that the social outcome of a technology is determined by the technology itself together with economics, whereas Weber would have pressed us to look beyond this and consider people's value systems and motives — that is, what *drives* them to act as they do?[92]

In this book I am clearly following the lead of Max Weber, for it has been argued that technology alone has no power whatsoever; it is dead-metal. The fact that it has certain 'liberties of action' to offer is something that is discovered by people, who find their own uses for it, people who have had their particular interests, desires, motives, and values shaped by the various institutions of their society; it is these which underly their decisions as to how the 'liberties of action' shall be adopted and put to use so as to meet what they feel to be their priorities of satisfaction.

8. Telecommunication May Not Reduce Travel in Future, But May Increase It

Another interesting matter that cannot be discussed adequately in terms of rationality alone is the question whether or not our expanding computer and telecommunication networks will gradually reduce the necessity for people to travel about so much. In its most extreme form, the vision that is sometimes conjured up is that of millions of office workers sitting at home with their computer

terminals and television screens, pushing buttons rather than travelling to work. Or it is that of house-bound housewives, armed with
supermarket catalogues, perhaps with their Prestel sets, sending out
their coded shopping orders to the supermarket, who may then send
out direct debit instructions to the customer's bank. The images are
horrific, void of all human contact, and need not detain us here.[93]

Undoubtedly, the great expansion of our telephone, telegraph
and computer networks has allowed many of our highly centralised
industrial units to be broken down into smaller units and these to
disperse around the country (e.g. many insurance houses). But this
is not dispersal and isolation of individuals, only of groups. There is
no question about the traditional patterns of travel to work being
radically changed; they certainly will be. Communication and transportation have always been linked. For example, the railways last
century were enabled to develop into an organised system only by
means of the telegraph, whilst today our airways can operate to
planned schedules only by virtue of our modern high-speed telegraph (e.g. Telex), and our shipping operates securely because of
radio. So far, the introduction of new communication systems has
systematically led to a vast *increase* in transportation traffic,
because it has rendered it increasingly possible and increasingly
secure.[94]

Our broadcasting services too, radio and television, have opened
people's eyes to the delights of foreign holidays, and packaged
tourism has flourished. Today we take it for granted that we can
travel on business or go on holidays abroad, with feelings of great
security. International and national conferences have both become
increasingly fashionable too, but is there any reason why 'teleconferencing' should replace them? It might be argued that economics
will decide for communication rather than for transportation in
future: but do we seriously believe that the planning of conferences
is based primarily on economic grounds? No, conferences are social
occasions. People join them to meet their colleagues, to get away
from the office for a few days, to enjoy a change of scenery and, let
it be confessed, because going to a conference can boost their feelings of importance. Again, it is usually cheaper to telephone your
friends then to travel to visit them, but to act always on that economic argument is the quickest way to lose your friends. There is a
world of difference between a person's real *presence* and his
disembodied image in sight and sound on a television set; the difference is not only psychological in nature but, above all, it lies in

the fact that your friend has seen you take the trouble to travel.[95]

It is my view that teleconferencing, far from substituting for real conferences, may possibly *increase* the number of conferences held in future, one reason being that the organisation of a conference is a lengthy and tedious task, when the members to be consulted arc widely scattered. A small, easily set-up, preliminary meeting could be held by using the teleconference system, so as to act as an organising meeting, thereby encouraging people to organise more conferences.

However, as regards the influence of communication and computer networks upon the pattern of travelling to work, it might be admitted that such arguments have less strength, because economic considerations will dominate the situation far more. These networks certainly offer the 'liberty of action' of enabling people to move from place to place, yet to function as though they were stationary (Section 5); that is to say, their existence offers this increased *choice* of activity, but does not necessarily enforce a particular pattern. If people are thereby offered the choice of staying at home with a computer terminal and video-telephone, or of travelling to work at the office with their colleagues and friends, their decisions will depend upon a host of factors other than any economic incentives which they may be offered to work at home — for example, the physical discomforts of their particular commuting needs, whether staff can be enrolled who are willing to operate one way or another, their morale at work, etc. It seems more likely, to me, that these networks certainly will encourage dispersal of large, city-based, enterprises, but that the new pattern emerging will be one of local offices or centres, where the necessary computer terminals and other equipment may be located. The problems of commuting would be lessened, whilst the workers' psychological needs for human company would still be satisfied. It would be work within a social context.

One point is quite clear: communication cannot literally *substitute* for transportation. As emphasised already in Chapter 1 (Section 6), when communicating (*communicare*) the partners are, in voice and mind, at both ends of the line simultaneously; they are 'mapped together'. But when commuting (*commutare*) they are not, but are exchanging their locations from one end to the other. Communication and transportation are then categorically distinct in the 'liberties of action' which they offer, so their functions are not logically equivalent. They cannot literally substitute for one another.

It may be true to say that the nineteenth century technologies of power — e.g. factories, with moving shafts and belts, the railways, the steam engine — encouraged urban conglomeration and growth of cities. But it would be naive to accept, without question, the idea that our twentienth century technologies of communication and information will necessarily reverse the process. Just because something is technically possible is no reason for believing that it will be carried out. For there are many other factors to be considered, legal ones in particular (land-tenure, rights of way, employment, property ownership) together with great housing problems, retraining problems, management problems, local versus central government problems, and as many mind-boggling political problems.

Notes

1. The words *political* and *policy* are used throughout in their general sense, to refer to people's choosing their actions with intent, according to their personal principles, so as to attain some desired ends ('Prudent conduct' in the *Concise Oxford English Dictionary*, 1976 edition). The words do not necessarily refer to 'the act of government', or to party politics.

2. Mr Colin Godman, Producer, BBC, Broadcasting House, Bristol.

3. See *Sociology and Philosophy*, E. Durkheim, translated by D.F. Pocock, and with an article on Durkheim's life and work by Talcott Parsons, The Free Press, New York, 1974. (First published, in French, in 1924).

4. Admittedly, there are no sharp boundaries between *invention* and *improvement*, but such broad classification can generally be made.

5. See Lecture (1) of Sir Edmund Leach (Ch. 1, note 12).

6. See Section 6 of Chapter 1.

7. E.C. Cherry (Ch. 1, note 46).

8. In the Weberian sense of that word. See Section 3, Chapter 1.

9. See the editor's introduction to I. de Sola Pool (Ch. 1, note 22). 'The Sociology of the Telephone', S.H. Aronson, *International Journal of Comparative Sociology*, *XII*, September 1971, 154.

10. See Lord Asa Briggs in I. De Sola Pool (Ch. 1, note 22) and 'Bell's Electrical Toy. What's the Use? The Sociology of Early Telephone Usage', S.H. Aronson, in the same volume.

11. The very first words spoken over a telephone (by Graham Bell) gave an order: 'Mr Watson, come here, I want to see you'.

12. These advertisements have been conveniently reproduced in the *Australian Telecommunication Research Journal*, *8 (2)*, 1974. They are also reproduced in E.C. Cherry, (Ch. 1, note 46).

13. The Aborigines presumably.

14. Italics mine (C.Cherry). It would seem that the 'men of high civilisation' could think of nothing better to say than could the 'perfectly uncivilised natives' — with the telephone to help them.

15. E.C.Cherry (Ch.1, note 46).

16. See S.H. Aronson (note 10), and 'The Birth and Early Years of the Bell Telephone System, 1876-1880', R.J. Tosiello, an unpublished doctoral dissertation

referred to by Aronson, ibid.

17. S.H.Aronson (note 10).

18. By 1876 there were nearly a quarter of a million miles of telegraph cable criss-crossing the USA, carrying 30 million telegrams per annum.

19. I.de Sola Pool (Ch.1, note 22).

20. E.C. Cherry (Ch. 1, note 46).

21. E.C. Cherry (Ch. 1, note 93).

22. See Section 5 of this chapter.

23. See the editor's comments on pp. 66-7 of I. de Sola Pool, (Ch. 1, note 22).

24. There is, of course, a certain number of telephones in private homes that are used for business purposes (e.g. industrial managers, stockbrokers, turf accountants, etc.)

25. E.C. Cherry (Ch.1, note 93).

26. For some historical accounts of early computers see *Babbage's Calculating Engines*, H.P. Babbage, Spon Ltd, London, 1889. *Calculating Machines and Instruments*, D. Baxendall, Catalogue of the Collection in the Science Museum, London, HMSO, 1926. *Calculating Instruments and Machines*, D.R. Hartree, University of Illinois Press, Urbana, 1949. *The Ultra Secret*, F.W. Winterbotham, Weidenfeld & Nicholson, London, 1974. *The Colossus*, B. Randall, University of Newcastle (UK). 'Science and Technology Report 90,' 1976. An abridged version appeared in *New Scientist*, *73*, 1977, 346. *Faster than Thought: a Symposium on Digital Computing Machines*, Baron Vivian Bowden, Pitman, London, 1957. Also, by the same author, (but not published), 'The Language of Computers', first Richard Goodman Memorial Lecture, Brighton College of Technology, UK, 2 May 1969.

27. See the works by F.W. Winterbotham and B. Randall in note 26.

28. See 'The Early Days of British Computers', S.H. Lavington, *Electronics and Power*, *1*, (I.E.E., London) November/December 1978, 2 January 1979.

29. [This seems a good place to add a note from Cherry's files (not earmarked for any particular chapter and headed 'needs rewording'). 'The rapidity of invention, design and redesign, etc., is today so great (at least within our present sphere) that the whole industrial development of micro-electronics, of radically new communication systems, of so-called "learning" systems, etc., is felt by many laymen, whose criticisms or expressed fears must ever be attended to by "experts", as constituting a major social threat'.]

30. See *Giant Brains, or Machines that Think*, E.C. Berkeley, John Wiley & Sons Inc., New York, 1949.

31. Baron Vivian Bowden, *Faster than Thought* (note 26).

32. Quoted here with the kind permission of Lord Bowden.

33. See note 35 below.

34. [It is worth pointing out here that Cherry has not made explicit the essential point which is not that the *image* of computers has changed in the 'public mind'(which is probable), but that the purposes to which they are put have changed. Many computers do not in fact do much computation, it seems to me. We have here another example of a technology coming to be used for purposes not originally envisaged, namely, information management and processing. We now have *calculators*, in sizes varying from wrist-worn to 'engines' of tremendous sophistication, and *processors*, also in varying sizes. The machines are occasionally indistinguishable but their functions must be kept in mind].

35. Previously known as 'Viewdata'. Such systems use the home or office telephone in conjunction with a domestic television receiver. Requests for information, on thousands of possible subjects, are dialled into a central computer and replies are presented on the screen, in the form of data, pictures, instructions, questions, etc. as needed.

36. See note 1.

37. This subject is taken up again in Section 6 of Chapter 3.

38. The popular name for micro-processors.

39. At that time (1811-12) trade unions in Britain were regarded as seditious and suppressed by government, which thereby appeared as protector of the employers and their machinery. Driven by despair, through low wages, unemployment and starvation, the 'Luddites' started smashing the machines until suppressed by the military. It was purely a local 'militant action' and offered no threat of revolution. See G.M. Trevelyan, (Ch. 1, note 21).

40. See Section 4 of this chapter. See also note 29.

41. J. McHale and M.C. McHale (Ch. 1, note 39).

42. See *Deschooling Society*, I. Illich. Harper & Row Inc., New York, and Calder & Bayars, London, 1971.

43. R.H. Tawney (Ch. 1, note 27).

44. See *Small is Beautiful: A Study of Economics as if People Mattered*, E.F. Schumacher, Blond & Briggs, London, 1973.

45. J.K. Galbraith (Ch. 1, note 50).

46. D. Gabor (Ch.1, note 31). J. Robertson, (Ch. 1, note 39). J. McHale and M.C. McHale (Ch. 1, note 39). E.F. Schumacher (note 44). D. Bell (Ch.1, note 31). *A Guide for the Perplexed*, E.F. Schumacher, Jonathan Cape, London, 1977. *The Limits to Growth*, D. Meadows, D.L. Meadows, J. Randers, and W.W. Behrens, Universe Books, New York and Earth Island Fress, London, 1972. *Societal Directions and Alternatives; (Information for Policy Design)*, M. Marien, Lafayette, New York, 1976.

47. J.B. Bury (Ch. 1, note 36).

48. J.McHale and M.C. McHale (Ch. 1, note 39).

49. See Section 5 of Chapter 1.

50. J.B. Bury (Ch. 1, note 36).

51. 'Social contact' here means having ability to share in decision-making, or to achieve some other mutual purpose, to be aware of doing so, and of one's own part in the process.

52. See Section 2.

53. See remarks in Section 2 of Chapter 1 about Durkheim's view of technology as a social phenomenon.

54. M. Weber (Ch. 1, note 24). R.Aron (Ch. 1, note 11).

55. [Further attention was to have been given to this point in Chapter 5. See also, *Pierce & Pragmatism*, W.B. Gallie, Pelican Books, Harmondsworth, UK 1952 (Dover, New York, 1966). E.C. Cherry (Ch. 1, note 78 — 'On Human Communication').]

56. See Section 1.

57. M. Weber (Ch. 1, note 24). (See also Section 4 of Chapter 3).

58. 'Rational' means as it seems to the actor, not to the observer.

59. R. Aron (Ch. 1, note 11).

60. Weber, writing in German, used the word *Herrschaft*, which as Raymond Aron points out (see note 59), is ambiguous in translation (= lordship, dominion, mastery, control, government, sovereign authority, power, command, employers of servants, persons of rank (see *Cassell's German and English Dictionary*, Cassell & Co. Ltd, London, 1943)). Talcott Parsons uses the word 'authority'; but 'domination' is used by Aron and this suits our purpose better here. Weber was concerned with the sources of acceptable authority of leadership, of course, not with the blind exercise of sheer might.

61. R. Aron (Ch. 1, note 11).

62. *So-called*, because all human societies are technological (tool-makers and tool users); it is only a matter of degree (see Secion 2 of Chapter 1).

63. L. Mumford (Ch. 1, note 3).

64. R. Aron (Ch. 1, note 11).

65. [A point which was to have been taken further in Chapter 4.]

66. Radio, as a technique, is of course sometimes used for bilateral telephony, in both civil and military spheres. It is radio *broadcasting services* that are referred to here, and which are unilateral. They do elicit group responses from their audiences, e.g. by 'listener surveys' (consensus feedback), but not significant and free individual responses.

67. See 'The Language of the Body: the Natural Environment of Words', R. L. Birdwhistell, in *Human Communication: Theoretical Explorations*, A. Silverstein (ed.), Lawrence Erlbaum Associates, New Jersey, 1974. *Communication in Face-to-Face Interaction*, J. Laver and S. Hutcheson, Penguin Books Ltd, Harmondsworth, UK, 1972. Two specific articles in this book are drawn to the attention of the reader: 'The Experimental Analysis of Social Performance' by M. Argyle and A. Kendon, and 'Eye Contact, Distance and Affiliation', by M. Argyle and J. Dean.

68. Even many deaf-blind people develop touch signs to an astonishing degree, enabling them to enjoy a social sense and life. [Cherry wrote to me on 15 May 1979 asking for authentic sources or references dealing with the social behaviour of deaf-blind people, in groups. I could provide none].

69. E. Durkheim (Ch. 1, note 47). R. Bierstedt (Ch. 1, note 10).

70. [Some of the problems of *meaning* were to have been deferred until Chapter 5.]

71. Nowadays it is usual for some person or persons to act as an audience in the studio, perhaps for this reason of introducing 'presence', even though those people do not speak.

72. It has been the experience of the British Post office that some popular broadcasts may stimulate hundreds of thousands of telephone calls, of which only a trivial number may be accepted for the programme. In spite of the special lines provided for this purpose, such sudden demand for calls may seriously interfere with normal telephone traffic. See 'The Phone-in Phenomenon', P.G. Archer and B. Egglestone, *Post Office Telecommunications Journal*, summer 1978.

73. For example, John Reith, the first managing director of the British Broadcasting Company wrote in 1925, that to use 'so great a scientific invention for the purpose of entertainment alone would be a prostitution of its powers and an insult to the character and intelligence of the people'. See *Broadcast over Britain*, J.C.W. Reith, Hodder & Stoughton, London, 1924. Also, Lord Asa Briggs (Ch. 1, note 61) and Sir Frederik Sykes (Ch. 1, note 62).

74. Postal services, for use by government or the military, are a very ancient concept. The first post was probably that of semitic Babylonia, about 3800 BC, and was followed by that of the Persians. The Roman Imperial Post (*Cursus Publicus*) served the purposes of military government throughout occupied Europe. It used horses and caravans, with regular staging posts, and was essential to the control of the scattered Empire. See *Essai sur la 'Cursus Publicus' sous le haut-empire romain*, H.G. Pflaum, Imprimerie Nationale, Paris, 1950. 'The Speed of the Roman Imperial Post', A.M. Ramsay, *Journal of Roman Studies, 15*, 1925, 60. Also, E.C. Cherry (Ch. 1, note 93).

75. This tradition started in Europe in the 13th century, when royal messengers conveyed letters for payment. In England a Postmaster-General was appointed in the year 1610, responsible for both inland and foreign mail. There followed great confusion as many rival post services, mostly short-lived, were operated, until the time of Oliver Cromwell and the Restoration. (See also Ch. 1, note 60). The office of Postmaster-General in the American Colonies was created in the year 1692, and in 1775 Benjamin Franklin was appointed, under the authority of the American Congress. (See *Encyclopaedia Brittanica*, under 'Post').

76. *Contemptuous*, because 'the masses' represents human beings as a kind of porridge (Greek, *maza* = barley meal). Thomas Carlyle (in 'Shooting Niagara, and After', in volume 7 of the collection cited in note 71 of Chapter 1, written in 1867) spoke of 'The masses. . .swarmery, buffoonery, sons of the Devil, blockheadism,

gullibility, amenability to beer and balderdash', so such contempt is not of modern origin; the expression goes back to the time of the French Revolution, at least.

77. See *Culture and Society, 1780-1950*, R. Williams, Chatto & Windus, London, 1958. Also, E.C. Cherry (Ch.1, note 93), Lord Asa Briggs, (Ch.1, note 61).

78. The two spheres of usage may often be distinguished by their differential tariff system.

79. E.C. Cherry (Ch.1, note 93).

80. 'Language-systems' are symbolic systems which use prescribed, or defined, rules (e.g. arithmetic). Human languages do not. [The reader was here referred to Chapter 5 'for discussion of their difference and of the theory of meaning'. See, however, Section 8 of Chapter 3].

81. E.C. Cherry, (Ch.1, note 46).

82. I. de Sola Pool (Ch.1, note 22).

83. See *A History of Engineering and Science in The Bell System, (The Early Years: 1875-1925)*, M.D. Fagen (ed.), Bell Telephone Laboratories, Inc., USA, 1975.

84. G.M. Trevelyan (Ch.1, note 21). L. Mumford (Ch. 1, note 3).

85. E.C. Cherry (Ch.1, note 46).

86. See Section 6 of Chapter 1.

87. [There was a reference here to an unwritten passage concerning an analogous and perhaps more serious problem posed by the "video telephone" '.]

88. E.C. Cherry (Ch. 1, note 93). I. de Sola Pool (Ch. 1, note 22).

89. See note 23.

90. See Section 2 of this chapter.

91. W.J. Baker (Ch.1, note 5), and W.P.Jolly ibid.

92. [A point to have been discussed further in Chapter 7.]

93. Whether or not such images will become reality depends wholly upon the forms of the social organisations which are set up to operate the technical possibilities. (See 'Alternatives EFT Developments and the Quality of Life (a Theoretical Analysis)', R. Kling, *Telecommunications Policy,* 341, March 1979, 52). The satisfaction that customers will feel, in a 'cashless society', using Electronic Funds Transfer systems, will depend upon their feelings about the powers that they have over the organising institutions (e.g. their feelings of choice, of control over correction of errors, of confidence in correctness of records, etc.) and so of their feelings of trust. Even with adequate protection by law and by good traditions there remains the danger that the abolition of physical cash and its substitution by abstract data records may leave the customer less protected against his rashness (e.g. as credit cards have led millions of people into debt).

94. E.C. Cherry (Ch.1, note 93).

95. [This particular subject was to have been taken up in Chapter 6. It raises the question as to whether a face on a television screen is seen by the viewer as a person or a thing.]

3 COMMUNICATION AND ITS TECHNOLOGY: THE LIMITS OF OBJECTIVITY

> An empirical science cannot tell anyone what he *should* do — but rather what he *can* do — and under certain circumstances — what he wishes to do. (Max Weber), *Objectivity in Social Science and Social Policy* (1904).[1]

Undoubtedly, one of the principal reasons why some people's thoughts are being directed towards the notion of a 'Second Industrial Revolution' is the special nature of today's 'information technology', with its apparent simulation of certain human mental processes and its seeming contrast to the power technology of earlier times. The public imagination was readily caught soon after World War II by reports of 'electronic brains', an expression that was soon happily dropped but, unfortunately, only to be replaced by another — 'machine intelligence'. We hear too, today, of 'machine re-cognition', which implies that the machine has cognitive powers in the first place; yet how can dead-metal have such powers? Again, there has been talk of machines which can play chess (and give you a very good game) yet — is there any reason why this should be a source of *wonder*? The rules of chess are defined.

Such activities today represent technological expressions of certain philosophical questions stemming from Descartes, especially questions of mindbody relationships. These fall into two sections: First, *man as machine* (since the body is a physical object, why does it not obey the laws of mechanics? Or, in the words of Julien de la Mettrie (1740) is the mind 'a necessary result of the organisation of the human machine?'). Secondly, *machine as man* (automata, robots; can machines be made that simulate human, purposeful behaviour?).

With regard to the latter, it is worth remembering that we, as human beings, make and use tools and machines for the very reason that they do not exactly simulate human abilities — but that they supplement and enhance these abilities.

In this chapter I will attempt to survey the field and to present reasons for believing that our human *social* activity of communicating with one another, *with understanding*, cannot possibly be explained wholly in the language of physical science, but that other categories of description are essential.

1. The Subjective and the Objective are United in Experience

The word *feeling* is used today in two distinct senses; feeling as *sensation* and feeling as *emotion*. The same distinction also seems clear to our modern minds when we think about our other senses — seeing, hearing, smelling, tasting. Nevertheless, sensation and emotion are united in experience. Thus, 'a nasty smell' is a single experience, not two separate ones, as indeed is 'a beautiful blue sky' or 'an harmonious chord' in music. We readily speak of the sensation itself and of the emotion it arouses as though they are separate; but to our modern minds they are separate only as concepts, although they cannot be as experiences. We cannot perceive 'beauty' other than in some beautiful object, any more than we can feel 'hatred' without there being something, real or imaginary, to hate; we can however speak about them *as though* we are able to do so.[2] In the most general way our perception of something, as an experience, inherently includes our valuation of it.[3] Or in existential terms, there must always be an essential nexus between ourselves and whatever we are attending to.

The historian R.G. Collingwood,[4] commenting upon this, has observed that things would have seemed quite different to people of medieval times. Referring to evidence of the colour-symbolism of their day, he stresses that they would not have been conscious of seeing some colour without feeling some corresponding emotion, and that, even today, neither do children nor artists.[5] The conceptual separation of sensation and emotion is a faculty of abstraction which our language and education instil in us today and it is an essential factor in our rational domination. Collingwood refers to this conceptual cleavage as 'sterilising' the sensa.

Objectivity has become a dominant ethic in the modern, 'scientific' world, and it requires us to hold the conceptual distinction between the so-called 'inner' and 'outer' worlds clear in our minds whilst our experience unites them. This is essentially an intellectual act, an act of *analysis* rather than of experience. Its origins lie in the Renaissance,[6] and it became clarified and dominant at about, say, the time of Erasmus (1466-1536).[7] It is true that Roger Bacon in the thirteenth century had come to believe in the necessity of experiment for understanding the 'outside' world of nature, and it was Leonardo (1452-1519), a contemporary of Erasmus, who actually put this idea into practice, whilst it was Galileo (1564-1642) who first established the basis of experimental method in science.[8]

Objectivity requires us to adopt an attitude of moral detachment in our thinking and reasoning, and it is essential both to the methodology and to the morality of science (but not to the choices that we make of our subjects for research nor to the uses to which we may apply the results). But this faith in objectivity was not something that came suddenly; it could only grow through the courage of many people, for it required them to break with tradition, especially with the tradition of scholasticism.[9] It required them to accept the limitations of introspection into the ideas of perfect forms, of God the mathematician, of the 'music of the spheres' and to come to accept that observation and experiment were necessary — that they were both rationally right and morally right. But in so doing they were skirting close to the slough of heresy.

The break from tradition implied by the growth of objectivity and the separation of the 'outer' world of nature from the 'inner' world of faith, morals and emotions, together with the new trust in experimentation (tampering with God's handiwork?) was first and foremost an act of immense courage and secondly a triumph of intellect. 'It is the customary fate of new truths to begin as heresies' wrote Thomas Henry Huxley, and he wisely continued: 'and to end as superstitions'.[10] Today we know well that science does not aim to establish permanent, immutable, truths, but that it is a quest which never ends; but the 'natural philosophers' of the fifteenth and even sixteenth centuries did not have that thought to comfort them.

2. Medieval Man and Renaissance Man: the Growth of Objectivity

It is very difficult for us today to understand the medieval mind (unless we happen to be historians). It was a mind that Sir William Dampier has described as being 'fascinated by a supposed analogy between the nature of the Godhead, the astronomical constitution of the Cosmos, or macrocosm, and the anatomical, physiological and psychological structure of man, the microcosm'. It was a mind enmeshed in an 'enormous and intertwined tangle of astrology, alchemy, magic and theology'.[11] It was a world in which everything was perceived as being symbolic.[12] The medieval mind was charismatically dominated by the Divine Plan, of which man himself was part, so that nothing that he did could possibly interfere with that Plan; his every action was felt to be part of it.[13]

The opening up of the medieval mind, during the early Renaissance, was due in the first place to the rediscovery of the writings of Aristotle,[14] and steady separation of the subjective and the objective was one of its eventual results.[15] Man came to a new feeling of liberation, of responsibility for his actions, of being able to question and challenge authority and to stand as an individual amongst his fellows. In so doing he necessarily had to separate himself from nature, to some extent, and so from the Divine Plan. He began to feel himself to be a being among other beings and objects *in* the world, the world 'outside' him, and less as being *of* the world, embraced by the Divine Plan with which God would allow no interference. The ground was being laid for the breakdown of scholasticism and for *experimental* science to flourish, a new science which could no longer be solely a matter of enquiry into the nature of the Divine Plan and its perfection, but which came to be seen as requiring man's intervention and interference; that is, through experimentation upon the 'outside' world, now 'external' to himself. Human action came to be something of immense significance and not, as to the medieval mind, something futile, helpless and without significance before the awesome face of the Divine Plan.

The radical transformation of medieval man into Renaissance man, and the subsequent flourishing of experimental science has often been called one of the greatest triumphs of the human intellect. However, in its early stages at least, it was rather a triumph of moral courage. Copernicus (1473-1543) and his contemporary Leonardo, like Galileo a century later (1564-1642), were devout Catholics, and their decisions and actions must have involved them in immense inner struggle to reconcile these with doctrine. They were not defiant rebels, flying in the face of the Church; God had given them minds with which to enquire and so it was their duty to do so, not in order to attack the Church but only some of its abuses and absurdities. We may perhaps see parallels in the modern world, in which certain courageous 'dissidents' are daring to challenge certain abuses and absurdities of political orthodoxy whilst, at the same time, being true patriots and adherents to the culture of their motherland.

Things are very different for us today. Separation of the objective from the subjective seems to offer us no problems, at least in our *analytic* thinking. Physical science depends upon this conceptual schism, for it requires us to reject all symbolism and all personal valuations in what we observe.

3. Neither Communication nor Technology are Wholly Understandable in Objective Terms Alone

'Politics is much more difficult than Physics' — who do you think said that? Some politician boasting of failing his exams when a schoolboy? No; it has been attributed to Albert Einstein.[16]

The word *difficult* is ambiguous. One's difficulty may be intellectual, or emotional, or physical, or pecuniary — many differing types; and the difficulties of politics are very different in kind from those of physics. Since Einstein's remark does not therefore compare like with like, what can it mean? This question might well be answered by saying that politics has brought more people to an early grave than has physics — and such an answer would not be facetious.

The science of physics, 'one of the greatest triumphs of the human mind', has succeeded in penetrating into such great depths of understanding of the 'physical' world by circumscribing its sphere of enquiry. Its methodology is based upon objectivity, and it is not concerned with subjective elements of human experience; it aims to exclude all questions of personal valuations — prejudices, biases, desires, but in so doing it ensures that it cannot be adequate for understanding in many other fields of human concern. It is not a question of it being right or wrong in those other fields; only that, if we seek to understand many of the social, political and other human problems which beset us today, we must go beyond physical science and introduce additional concepts into argument. Physical science is most powerful, above all, for dealing with *what*? and *how*? questions, but it can offer far less help to us for dealing with *why*? questions.

The great pioneers of physical science, Galileo above all, were most active in astronomy and mechanics,[17] and the foundations were built upon the primary concepts of mass, length and time. Astronomy involved observation and calculation, but necessarily left experimentation to Nature herself, with her eclipses and other happenings; mechanics could be helped by experiments in the laboratory. The technology necessary for measurement of mass, length and time had existed for a long time, but the needs of the new philosophy encouraged great improvement in its design. Chemistry too flourished and partly for similar reasons: that the experimental method became established and the technologies were refined. So too with all branches of physical science that evolved later, thermodynamics, electricity and magnetism, chemical synthesis —

all flourished upon their foundations of objectivity, leaving understanding of psychological, economic, linguistic, moral, social, and political problems trailing far behind, for these all require consideration of values, in various ways (although this is not to be assumed as being the reason for this historical fact).

It will be our argument here that, in addition, neither human communication nor technology itself can be understood wholly in objective terms. Both are essentially social activities; communication is the primary social act, the act of sharing between two or more persons,[18] whilst technology is social activity in the Durkheimian sense.[19] We understand a tool or a machine, *per se* (and not merely as an object or thing) not in the objective terms of physics, but only through the meaningful actions that it enables us *to carry out*; it is our activities which make it a tool or a machine.

The various objects in this world that come to our attention are sharply divided by us into two classes: (a) 'natural objects' (sticks, stones, trees, clouds) and (b) artefacts (houses, automobiles, clothes), and our psychological responses to the two are quite distinct. When archaeologists go on a dig, they turn up stones and rocks of random shapes and sizes and then suddenly, an object is unearthed which they recognise immediately as being different — say a piece of Roman pottery. But what distinguishes this interesting artefact from the stones and lumps of clay, its shape?

This may seem a silly question to ask; any fool knows the difference. However, if we interpret the expression 'random shapes' literally, that would include the object of pot-shape with probability equal to that of any other *specific* shape. The question is not quite as silly if, for 'Roman pot' we substitute 'neolithic axe-head', for it may then take an expert eye to spot the difference between this and the other chipped flintstones lying about. How does our expert do it?

The archaeologist himself might give several answers, in terms of his previous experience of such objects. But, essentially, it comes down to recognising that that particular stone could only have been chipped into shape by some neolithic man, and intended to be used by him *as* an axe-head. The expert could possibly make one like it and use it similarly;[20] he could, *as it were*, put himself in the place of the neolithic man. However, there is more to it than this; because the archaeologist cannot *be* a neolithic man in all aspects of his thinking and feeling — he can only interpret what he finds through his own, present-day, knowledge, attitudes and skills.[21]

This distinction between our understanding of nature and of man-made artefacts is very important when we consider today's 'information technology', because of the appearance that it often gives of simulating human mental processes. We hear frequently about machines that can learn, and of computers taking over what had previously been regarded as essentially human mental tasks; various traditionally 'white collar' employments are threatened, and there is a certain public alarm as to what 'machine intelligence' may do to us in the near future. What is the truth behind all this?

In the seventeenth century there was a not dissimilar concern aroused by the new philosophy, experimental science, which then seemed to threaten traditional religious life and institutions. Man was separating himself from God; there were problems about 'free will' and what man could do and what only God could do, or what could be understood or not. One philosopher who made striking clarification of such concerns (but who attracted little attention in his day) was Giambattista Vico, and his ideas are most relevant to our situation today.

4. The Doctrine of Giambattista Vico; the Man-made World and the Natural World

It was the historian and philosopher Giambattista Vico of Naples (1668-1744) who was the originator of the doctrine which holds that in order for us really to understand anything, and not merely to know about it, it is necessary that we should have made it.[22] Understanding involves creative activity, not necessarily creation of some material artefact, but equally the construction of abstract 'models', theories, structures in words or in symbols (as in mathematics). Vico was himself particularly concerned with law and with history, though his doctrine may be widely applied, even to technology — as it has been.[23] He saw history as being made in men's minds, as creative human activities, as construction within the human mind — and so, for that reason, understandable.

In the words of Sir Isiah Berlin:

What is altogether his own is the notion of history as the continuous, self-transformation of man and of human institutions in the course of man's struggles to overcome human and natural obstacles which, because it is the activity of men and the consequences of human structures, can be understood by men, understood as nature cannot be. This is his own: it is this original doctrine that. . .gained the admiration of. . .Marx.[24]

In adopting this view Vico took a stance against Descartes, who held that because history could never be precise it could not be accepted as true knowledge; true knowledge, he argued, was attainable only by the exact methods of mathematics and physics.[25]

From the viewpoint of the Vico doctrine we may be said to understand technological artefacts because we make them. But we cannot be said really to understand nature because we have not made it. Nature is not man's handiwork, but God's. That is, we can never understand nature *in toto*, but only in limited ways through our ability to create 'models', which we can understand.[26] We each of us are taught to regard nature in our different ways, according to our cultures, education and experiences; thus I have my own limited understanding of nature, whilst an Eskimo, say, may have different views, for we are likely to have built different models in our heads, through our differing experiences and our different needs. It is our models that we really understand, not nature itself, because we have made them.

Now the word *model* may suggest to some readers the idea of a mechanical construction. However, 'models' may be either real or abstract. Many early scientific models were certainly mechanical (e.g. early atomic models and models of the 'aether') because mechanics was an early science. Models may be abstract, conceptual models; nevertheless, they are (mental) human *constructions*, and it is these constructions that are knowable and understandable — because man has constructed them. The physicist, for example, constructs his models out of his chosen elemental concepts and the complex mathematical relations between them; it is these models that he really understands, not nature itself.

In our ordinary, everyday lives we each of us carry in our heads our own constructed models of the world, and it is these which we understand and adjust to. Such models are then shareable with others like ourselves, of comparable experiences, languages and cultures — that is, they are communicable. We understand 'one-another', to that extent.

If such a doctrine is accepted, then it follows that our understanding of the natural world can be elaborated only by elaborating our models, building into them yet further elements. But we have no reason to believe that there can ever be finality to this process, giving us full understanding of nature,*in toto*; there will always be some ultimate lacuna, lying beyond the limits of existing knowledge. Furthermore, there is no reason to believe that we each create single unified models, which give us understanding. This may be an ideal within some specific fields of thought such as logic; I do not know. But even physics uses a plurality of models. In our everyday life we may build many models, giving us different kinds of understanding in different circumstances, or when identifying with different groups of people. Nor need our various models be consistent, for our needs may vary in these different circumstances.

However, if we wish to undersand how human beings communicate, it is certain that a plurality of scientific models will be needed, for we are then dealing not only with physical understanding but with psychological and social understanding too. Let us next take a quick glance at some of the historical background of these disciplines, both of which have been influenced by physics and its methodology, but which require us to go beyond physics conceptually because they are both concerned with human beings — and the scientist-observer is one of them himself; he is both subject and object, knower and known.

5. Some Historical Notes — Subjectivity in the Human Sciences

The *Concise Oxford English Dictionary*[27] defines the word 'objective' as

> Belonging not to the consciousness or the perceiving or thinking subject but to what is presented to this, external to the mind, real . . .(of persons. . .) dealing with outward things, exhibiting actual facts uncoloured by exhibitor's feelings or opinions. . .

However, the concept 'external to the mind' raises epistemological problems, concerning the 'inside' and 'outside' worlds; for whereas all experience (awareness, perceptions, thoughts, feelings) is ultimately mental, to say that something is 'in the mind' is nonsense, because it implies that there is something else (the 'external') which is 'not in the mind'. That can only mean either (a) 'it is in someone else's mind', or (b) that 'it does not exist' either in experience or imagination. Hence, the expressions 'inside world' and 'outside world' cannot refer to anything inside or outside 'the mind'; there is no such boundary. Neither do they mean inside or outside one's skin. They can only denote two classes of knowledge — (i) knowledge that is individualistic, regarded as private to each of us, such knowledge as we have about our own feelings and thoughts, and (ii) knowledge that we assume as having the possibility of being public, shareable with our fellows — i.e. as communicable.

From this point of view, the terms 'inside world' and 'outside world' distinguish, not two kinds of existence (physical/mental), but two kinds of knowledge — what is incommunicable and what is, in principle communicable.[28]

Sociology, psychology, and these other fields of enquiry apart from physical science, are concerned with people rather than with inanimate objects. They necessarily require us to consider what the dictionary refers to as 'the consciousness or the perceiving or thinking *subject*', and it has been the responsibility of these fields to develop methodology that is soundly scientific (i.e. that it may specify precise conditions of observation and experiment such that other people may be able to reproduce the results) that it should be *rational* and objective, even though subjective experience is involved. The important thing is to distinguish between scientific concepts and scientific method. Sociology, psychology, linguistics and these fields other than physical science have the need for additional basic concepts, because they are not dealing with inanimate objects but with people — and 'the observer' is a person too.

Perhaps the reader will excuse me if we make a very brief excursion into (potted) history.

The word *sociologie* was first used by the Frenchman Auguste Comte in 1839, and it was he who took the view that societies were not static, fixed organisations, but were in a state of continual development. Early social thinking had regarded 'society' as being more or less synonymous with 'the State', and its study as being the study of politics, for its foundations rested upon the works of Plato and Aristotle.

Comte was writing before the publication of Darwin's *The Origin of Species* in 1859, and it was the ideas which this work stimulated that had such profound effects upon social thinking at that time and later. Society came to be viewed as evolutionary too, as developing in ways that adapted it to the environment. Herbert Spencer, in particular, compared society with the living organism itself in some detail, by analogy. The theory of natural selection as a dynamic theory of the life process seemed to provide also a wonderful way of interpreting social theory, as the dynamics of the social process.

One of the profound effects of this was to reverse the earlier viewpoint of Auguste Comte which regarded society as being understandable by study of the individual human mind, through the highly subjective process of introspection; rather, the individual mind came to be regarded as developing out of the social process. Society is far greater than the sum total of the individuals whom it comprises, for the simple reason that these individuals are in some state or other of *organisation* (their division of labour, their governmental system, their bureaucracies, etc.). Society is essentially people in meaningful relationship; 'society' means 'people in communication'.[29]

Darwin himself wrote that the dynamic processes of 'advanced' (industrial) societies could not so easily be explained in terms of natural selection, because they have created institutions which protect the weak and the helpless: asylums, hospitals etc. and today including all those institutions of the welfare state, insurance offices, the police, education and others so familiar to us. Human society is dynamic, in a continual state of change; there is no logical reason to accept finality — for better or worse. Man's creative powers seem to have no *logical* end, neither for invention of new technology, nor for creation of other forms of social institution.[30]

The thinker who first set out to put sociology on a scientific base of methodology, whilst accepting that people's objectives, decisions and values are their own responsibilities, was Max Weber.[31] In Professor Aron's words

Weberian Science is defined. . .by an effort to understand and explain the values men have believed in . . .How can there be an objective science — one not distorted by our value judgements — of the value-charged productions of men? This is the central question Weber asked himself and to which he tried to provide an answer.[32]

Max Weber realised that scientific research could lead to no fixed, immutable laws; he saw it correctly as a quest which never ends — which is as true of physics as of sociology. He pressed that subjectivity could not be denied, but that the researcher should not himself project his own value judgements upon what he observes. Social relationships are *meaningful* relationships, [33] though our immediate impressions of them may misinterpret their true nature or the true reasons for social behaviour patterns; we may indeed not even know the true reasons for much of our own behaviour. In fact it might be quite false to speak of *true* reasons, for these are unknowable; only patient observation, factual data and analysis may lead us far closer to the reasons than will introspection. Max Weber's aim, in establishing sociology as a science, was to accept that people's social behaviour and the varied institutions which they create are value-directed, and to take due account of this when attempting to explain *why* social behaviour is as it is. Social science, in Weber's view, is distinguished from physics by the need to reckon with this subjective element (although there are other distinctions too).

Turning now to psychology, we find that this also had its beginnings in philosophical enquiry,[34] as it sought to establish itself as a new discipline involving concepts that were excluded from physical science, which dealt with inanimate phenomena. In the eighteenth and early nineteenth centuries it was emerging from philosophy and metaphysics, out of the thinking of Kant, Locke, Hume, Berkeley and others. The early problems were epistemological — concerned with concepts like 'ideas', 'mind', 'associations', 'understanding', and with the 'mind/body problem'. It was recognised that, as a science, it necessarily differed from physical science, for it was directed towards understanding not of the 'outside world' but rather of the individual's own experiences. There was therefore no 'external' object of enquiry; it was, in its various schools, defined as being subjective and individualistic whereas the physical sciences were objective and universalistic.

By the middle of the nineteenth century the methods of physical science were having a profound influence, and *psychophysics* developed. Psychology became increasingly experimental in the hands of people like E.H. Weber, Helmholz, Wundt, Bain and others, especially stimulus/response psychology. Methodology developed further, but the need to include concepts external to physics was established. Psychology, as an experimental science, requires the observer to experiment upon and study something that is of the same nature as himself — viz. human.[35] Clearly, there are moral bounds to the type of experimentation that he can perform. There is, in addition, the fact that human beings when situated in a laboratory and acting as experimental subjects may feel and behave differently from real life. They might even 'cheat' and defeat the scientists' purposes. The overcoming of such problems is a question of good methodology, of taking into account such matters as motivation or conditioning, or controlling of attention, of distinguishing reflex actions from wilful actions (choice, conation), etc. Nevertheless, the methodology can be rational and objective based upon formulation of hypotheses, tests and observations (especially using statistical methods).

The conditions and difficulties inherent in the very nature of psychological studies (experimental or not) have resulted not in its slow progress, which would be quite untrue, but rather in its abundant researches and applications becoming diversified into a number of distinct schools, — introspective psychology, behaviourism, Gestalt psychology, psychoanalysis and many others. These schools may be said to differ in their aims and objectives, their fields of enquiry and even in their different metaphysical assumptions. On the other hand physics, although it cannot be said to be a single monolithic structure, has not diversified into distinct schools.[36]

During the first half of this century physics proved to be so successful in dealing with inanimate phenomena that it came to exert a dominating influence over experimental psychology, which is, in one sense, more difficult than physics as regards its methodology. Psychology came to be widely accepted as the study of behaviour, rather than of 'the mind'; however, behaviourism did not regard the experimental subject as an inanimate object, nor did it deny all meaning to subjective concepts; rather it concentrated upon experiments into behaviour, as being truly observable, because it is both quantifiable and measurable, in the traditions of physical science. Following World War II this movement to draw experimental psychology closer to physics was taken further by some researchers, with the aim of establishing scientific laws of behaviour analogous to those of physics, which would enable them to predict human behaviour, as physical laws enable us to predict the behaviour of the inanimate world.[37]

However, it would appear that humans and other living creatures do not behave in quite the same way as inanimate objects. For example, if you were rash enough to kick me downstairs there is little doubt that my body would fly through the air in a trajectory that could be described by Newton's Laws of Motion. But such laws could not possibly describe what might happen next — for example, I might run up the stairs and start a fight.[38] Why? Physics cannot tell us, for it is not very good at dealing with *Why?* questions.

Why? questions are answered by the word: 'Because. . .' Because of what? The laws of physics and bodily chemistry? But bodies, animate or inanimate, do not move as they do *because* of scientific laws. Scientific 'laws' are man-made, like the laws of the land, but they do not cause the movements, nor can they be said to be *obeyed* by the physical objects. It is rather we who obey them, or at least conform to them, when we *describe* the regularities observed in nature.

If instead of asking *why* I ran upstairs to start a fight, we sought instead only for a means to describe, or specify, or predict that general class of behaviour, we might still find the need to introduce words that are not used in the language of physics — words like *purpose, intention*, or even words like *choice* or *decision*, or perhaps the ambiguous word *meaning*.[39] So let us now take a brief look at why this might be.

6. On the Deceits of Absolute Materialism

If the reduction of psychology to physics be pursued as an ideal and all reference to cognitive elements is banished we would end up with what may be called *absolute materialism*. Words like *intent, meaning, value, choice, belief, understanding*, etc. would find no place in explanations of human and animal behaviour that were offered. They would either be replaced by specific neuro-chemical activities, assumed to be their cause, or else the field of physics would have to be so enlarged and the conventional meaning of the word 'physical' so changed, as to encompass them. As things are at present, these cognitive terms (intent, meaning, etc.) are of a category quite distinct from physical terms, as distinct as form is from matter; even more distinct[40] for, say, the meaning of an utterance is not a property of that utterance but involves the relationship of that utterance *to* a specific person, at a particular moment in time, *in* a specific situation.[41]

Absolute materialism, if it is pursued as an ideal, either reduces human beings to the status of physical objects, to overwhelmingly complex assemblages of neurons, chemicals, tissue and bones, or else must needs introduce some new physical element that distinguishes the two. If the first be the case, then there seems to be no place for morals — but it is noticeable that even the most materially minded people do not treat their spouses, families and friends as though they were things — usually; unfortunately, with more remote relationships, or under conditions of great stress, or in war, the moral distinction between persons and things may crumble or even vanish. Anyone who professes belief in absolute materialism in this sense, reduces himself to the status of a slave owner; for that is what a slave is — a person treated as an object.[42]

Absolute materialism would require that all explanation of human behaviour is to be sought in the structure and physical operations of the brain and body. So what, it might be asked, has happened to the mind, to what Professor Gilbert Ryle has called the 'Ghost in the machine'?[43]

Ryle referred to this as 'Descartes's Myth', the bifurcation of a sensate creature into a body *and* a mind. However, absolute materialism has no place for mind at all; if anyone can be said to have originated the idea of absolute materialism it was not Descartes, but Julien de la Mettrie. René Descartes[44] was one who regarded physics and mathematics as being the only ways to certain truth, although he was also concerned about certain metaphysical and theological consequences of his own conclusions. He regarded animals as mindless automata, whereas human beings consisted of *both* bodies *and* minds, two separate things, acting independently, pursuing separate existences, yet appearing to operate together in a correlated manner. The body, being physical, should act according to the laws of physics — and yet, in practice, it obviously did not behave that way; it behaved as though controlled by part of the mind (the will). However, because Descartes regarded the body and the mind as being independent entities this produced a dilemma which he never succeeded in resolving.[45] This dualism led to the so-called 'mind/body problem', which has continued to be with us persistently ever since his day.

If absolute materialism be interpreted literally to mean seeking to understand human (or animal) behaviour entirely through study of the brain, and by creating scientific 'models' of its known physical properties, it would not exactly represent a revival of 'Descartes's Myth'; for it would exclude all references to cognitive factors. So in what ways may such a viewpoint be challenged?

At this point some readers must be saying to themselves: 'Of course the brain is physical; is this fellow trying to tell us that the brain is not made of meat?' No, I am not; I've frequently eaten brains — they are very nourishing (that is, sheep's brains). The real question is how, if we regard a human being (or animals for that matter) as a mechanism, as we ordinarily understand that word, can we account for human behaviour as being so different from that of inanimate objects — or even from that of animals?

The basic error of absolute materialism is that it is absolutely materialistic. As such it can only seek to understand nature in terms of 'what it is', in terms of reality itself, whereas it may be better to ask: 'what is knowable about it?' After all, the whole of what we know about nature is brought to us through our sense experiences, and by our internal reflections upon that experience.[46] Such knowledge must be expressed in language or in language systems, but there is no *a priori* reason why this must be confined to the language of physics. Other categories of language may be preferable (e.g. that of psychology). With these systems of expression, 'models' (theories, descriptions, explanations) may be built — and it is these that we can understand.

7. 'Man as Machine' Contrasted with 'Machine as Man'

The materialistic view that was referred to in Section 6 is only one such view; there is another which is, in a certain sense, diametrically opposed to it and which is, in my opinion, of far greater *practical* importance today. What was referred to before as *absolute materialism* was of religious importance in the seventeenth century (and even up to the nineteenth century in certain ways) because it raised questions about 'free will', of how the mind could exist in a material body, and whether this could be the result of some special quality of the material itself, or whether (as Julien de la Mettrie said) it was the result of the organisation of the human machine. Such questioning was mainly directed at what is or is not the case (what reality *is*). It was John Locke who turned the questioning towards what we can *know* about the case — and, more important, *understand* about it.[47]

Absolute materialism may be regarded as the result of taking an *analytic* view, of trying to understand what we do not understand (human, or even animal, behaviour) in terms of what we do understand — namely technology and physics. In summary, it may be regarded as trying to understand *man as machine*.

The alternative materialistic view is today of economic, industrial and political interest. This will here be termed *robotics*. This denotes a wide field of modern technology (computer, automata, 'mechanised intelligence' — 'the chip', etc.) which seemingly carry out certain forms of human task which previously had been widely thought to require human intelligence; it is claimed that these devices can *learn, predict, memorise, recognise, design,* etc. However, they are dead-metal, so how can any real meaning be attached to the expression 'mechanised intelligence'? This seems to me to be an unfortunate choice of words, partly because it is not clear what 'intelligence' really is; on any common-sense interpretation of the word it cannot be said to be a specifically human quality, for do not animals show similar qualities? So we shall avoid the loaded expression 'mechanised intelligence' here and speak of 'robotics' instead, without prejudice. It will be argued later[48] that *understanding* is the more essentially human characteristic.

If anyone seriously asks the question whether a technology can ever be created which shows any sign of essentially human mental activity, that technology should be called 'mechanised understanding' and that would certainly give good cause for eyebrows to be raised!

In contrast to absolute materialism, robotics is the result of taking a *synthetic* view of the man/machine relationship and, as remarked earlier, this seems to represent a materialist viewpoint which is of considerable practical importance today owing to its economic and political implications. However, it is my own opinion that it raises no new philosophical questions at all, nor does it contribute anything to clarification of the 'mind/body' problem.

In summary, robotics may be regarded as seeking the limits of information technology through the conceptual model of *machines as man*.

At the opening of this Section the remark was made that absolute materialism and robotics are, as ideas, diametrically opposed to one another, in a certain sense. Absolute materialism was of philosophical interest in earlier centuries, which has left us with a certain inheritance still, whereas robotics is more of practical, industrial, concern today.

The two ideas (man as machine and machine as man) are easily confused. As the expression has been used here 'absolute materialism' is taken to signify the idea that, because man is a physical object, his whole behaviour ought to be explicable in the language of physical science; it was argued that this idea contains a source of error and that, rather than ask what the brain is or is not, it would be better, if, instead, we enquired into what is *knowable* or *unknowable* about it.

Living creatures do not conform to the laws of dynamics in their behaviour as inanimate objects do (a puzzle which Descartes could not resolve); the question then raised by absolute materialism becomes: what is knowable about the physical properties of the brain which may enable us to account for this uniqueness of animate behaviour? The conclusion that will be drawn later (Section 8) is that the language of physics cannot be adequate for discussing such a question, and that other categories of description are needed (e.g. psychological and social).

On the other hand, the term 'robotics' is here taken to refer to that class of information technology which, so it is sometimes said, appears to simulate some aspects of what is commonly regarded as mental activity.

But mental activity is not something that we can observe with our senses, directly; it is behaviour that we observe. 'Mental activity' terms (cognition, meaning, intent, etc.) refer to factors which are unobservable; they are rather postulates that are introduced for the purpose of *explaining* human, or animal, behaviour.[49] It would then be better to say that this particular class of information technology, robotics, appears to simulate certain aspects of human *behaviour*, without reference to 'mental activity' or to any cognitive terms at all. For we know the structure of the machines, having made them, and so understand them; but we do not know the structure of human brains, because we have not made them and cannot be said really to understand them in the sense that we understand machines. Thus, there seems to be no logical reason why cognitive terms need be used, nor any reference made to mental activity when explaining their apparent simulation of some aspects of human behaviour.

These two materialist views may then be contrasted in the following way.

(1) Absolute materialism implies observing human or animal behaviour and then inferring an entirely physical (material) structure which would explain that behaviour without introduction of any cognitive terms whatever. It will be argued in Section 8 that such an absolutely material view cannot reveal any explanation of human communicative behaviour and that certain crucial aspects of human communication are explicable only if cognitive terms are also introduced — notably *conceptualisation* and *understanding*.
(2) With robotics it is the other way round. We know, or observe, the structure of the machines and infer their behaviour,

with the aim of simulating certain elements of human behaviour. We may be said to really understand such machines (in ways that we cannot be said to understand human beings) even those as complex as computers, because they are man-made (according to the Vico doctrine). Nevertheless, their detailed, moment-by-moment actions may not necessarily be precisely calculated (especially if a 'random element' be built into them);[50] we can then but infer their likely behaviour. It is my view that there is no need whatever to introduce cognitive expressions into explanation of the workings of 'robotic' machines or into that of any other information technology. Indeed, such introduction seems to be both anthropomorphic and confusing. The purposes of such technology are practical and industrial.

The fact that machines can be made which can give you a good game of chess, or which can even learn to do so, or which can 'recognise' patterns (even those of speech or writing) or can perform any other perceptual tasks may well surprise or even astonish people. But what is important is that these facts should not be a source of *wonder*.

At several points in the preceding Sections it has been urged that, whenever any comparison is made between brains and machines, or when the 'mind/body' problem is considered, it is better not to ask what the brain *is* or what the mind *is*, but rather to enquire into what is knowable or unknowable about them, and into what category of language (or 'universe of discourse') that knowledge is expressible. However, if we are to do this for the purpose of trying to understand *human*, as distinct from animal, communication, then it is into man's propositional language and human understanding that we should enquire. We are returned all the time, to the problems of language, of symbolism and of meaning.

8. Human Understanding: We Conceive Universals but Perceive only Particulars

Auguste Comte (1798-1857) considered that it was first necessary to study the workings of individual minds, through introspection, before their interactions within society could be understood. But it was later realised that this was putting the cart before the horse and that it would be more realistic to regard the individual mind as being the results of the social process.

To study individual adult minds is to study something already formed out of its social experience, not raw material; again, if a very young child born in one community be transferred to another community, it will develop through the language, customs and institutions of its hosts, in however rebellious a manner.

The same point may be taken at the neurophysiological level. No amount of study of one single brain, in total isolation, can possibly justify our inferring what will happen, in detail, when it is brought into conjunction with other brains. To understand what might happen, and why, would require us also to consider the nature of the interactions between them. That is to answer the question: How does one brain causally affect another?

Inter-actions between human beings are sometimes physical — unfortunately violently so. But for most of the time their interactions are not physical; they are symbolic. For instance, you are reading the words on this page and, whatever your reactions may be, they have not been physically caused by my handwriting, nor by the printer's ink. The words are completely empirical in shape.[51] They have been symbolically caused by my intentions and your interpretations.[52] Now there is no reason for believing that a human brain has preference for learning one particular language (or other sign-usage) any more than another.[53] The language that any particular person comes to acquire, and his meaningful usage of it among his fellows is essentially a *social* phenomenon; what is born into each of us is the drive to learn language of some kind and to develop social sensibilities of some sort,[54,55] which no doubt may eventually be given physical explanation, in terms of neurophysiology, chemistry, genetics, etc.

The forces of inter-action between human beings are, for most of the time, not physical but symbolic (linguistic, meaningful, significative) and symbolic causes belong to a universe of discourse which is quite distinct from that of physical science; symbolic cause and physical cause are categorically distinct. The main question then is this: is it conceivably possible that the meaning of spoken utterances, or of written sentences or of any other sign usage (empirical or iconic) can be reduced to wholly physical terms — even if the word 'physical' has to be widened in its interpretation? For, if so, the categorical distinction vanishes and the way would be wide open to developing a wholly physical science of human communication or even, if we let our fancy wander further still, a physical science of society.

I do not believe this to be possible, but that such a view could only be based upon a category error, for logical reasons that will be outlined here, provided that the words 'human communication' be interpreted at the highest level, to involve *understanding*, and not merely at the level of factual data, or of 'knowing that such-and-such is true or false', or of perceiving that something has been said, or written or otherwise expressed. That is to say, involving our phenomenal human powers of *conceptualisation* and understanding and not merely our powers, shared with the animals, of making perceptual abstractions.

Human understanding arises from our powers of forming concepts, and it is the nature of human language that provides the evidence we need of man's conceptual thought,[56] and it is the apparent absence of such evidence in animal communicative signing that justifies our assuming that they have neither conceptual thought nor understanding.[57] But their behaviour does show that they may not only perceive, and discriminate between, objects presented to their senses, but also that if any group of objects possesses a number of perceptible characteristics in common, the animal may demonstrate a 'disposition' to respond to any one of them as being the same (e.g. any member of its own species). Mortimer Adler refers to this as *perceptual abstraction*. Such processes in the animal are physical processes, and it is not to be wondered at that a computer may be programmed so as to do something rather similar; for example, to 'recognise' handwritten words [58] and to express them in typescript, with varying degrees of success (depending upon how many characteristics can be identified that are held in common by many samples of the handwriting).

But such perceptual abstraction, common to man and animals, does not approach the essentially human faculty of conceptualisation — the basis of understanding. The two processes are radically distinct and should not be confused, for such confusion can lead one either to the anthropomorphic view that animals (or even machines) can engage in abstract, conceptual thought; or else that human abstract, conceptual thoughts and understanding, together with propositional language, are no more than an advanced development of the animal faculty of perceptual abstraction. It may be meaningful to speak of animals' behaviour as showing evidence of *perceptual thought*, and even of rationality, but confined to what is being immediately perceived (which can only be a particular object, an individual, and not a class of objects). To quote from John Locke, writing in 1689:

> beasts compare not their ideas farther than some sensible circumstances annexed to the objects themselves. The other power of comparing which may be observed in man, belonging to *general* ideas, and useful only to *abstract* reasonings, we may probably conjecture beasts have not. [italics mine][59]

Locke is not here saying that beasts can 'compare' objects (i.e. relate them in any way) only whilst they are actually perceiving them, and that they cannot do this also from memories of the objects when they are absent. He is rather first saying that beasts can only perceive, or visualise and 'compare' *particular* objects and not 'general ideas' (*universals*). He is then saying that man can do this too, but that he can also go much further, into the new mode of *conceptualisation* of general classes, universals, or what he calls 'general ideas'. Without this human faculty language would be impossible, for the absence of all classification would require there to be a different name for everything, real or imaginary, for every experience, and for every different configuration or relationship into which these could be set; the names would be arbitrary and unrelated, for there could be no syntax.

It is the fact that human language is syntactically structured, together with the fact that vocabularies are finite, which provide evidence of man's phenomenal powers of abstraction at the conceptual level.

> Brutes abstract not [wrote John Locke] . . .for it is evident we observe no footsteps in them of making use of general signs for universal ideas. . .that they have not the faculty of abstracting or making general ideas, since they have no use of words or any other general signs.[60]

One of the remarkable things about human language, as it is used in everyday chatter, gossip, discussion and pleasantry, is that none of the words used are *defined*. So how does anyone really know what anyone else is talking about? Such general, everyday, linguistic expression, which we learn from the cradle onwards will here be called *ordinary language*. On the other hand, at times, we also employ certain specialised 'languages' which essentially do use definitions — that of physical science, for example. Such formal, deliberately constructed ways of expressing ideas within some specific field of interest are called *language-systems*. Thus mathematics is not 'a language', but a language-system. Similarly the 'rules of the road', which are assumed to be familiar to every motorist, form an elementary language-system; the various traffic signs are defined in the Highway Code book and they are not (as would sometimes seem to be the case) open to free interpretation by the motorist!

We are here concerned only with ordinary language, with which ordinary mortals communicate, one with another, unguided by any definitions or knowledge of syntactic rules.[61] How can such language work?

We humans seem to share with the beasts powers of making 'perceptual abstractions' and, if we had no faculty of language and could go no further than they, we should, presumably, live in the same kind of here-now world as the beasts. We both may perceive, and group together, objects that are similar in specific respects; we may discriminate between them — when they are presented to our vision or other senses (or even, to limited extent, in their memory). But the images that we see, or hear, etc., are always *specific* or *particular*. For example, if you hear someone say 'Please pass me a chair' the image seen in your mind's eye is of some particular chair. It is a percept; you can see, or hear, or imagine only such *particulars*, but not generalities or universals.[62] To deny that the creatures can have experience beyond that of perception of particulars is not to deny them any powers of reason at all, but it is to confine them to perceptual thought. To quote John Locke again:

> For if they have any ideas at all, and are not bare machines (as some would have them) we cannot deny them to have some reason. It seems as evident to me that they do, some of them, in certain instances, reason, as that they have sense; but it is only in particular ideas, just as they received them from their senses. They are, the best of them, tied up within these narrow bounds, and have not (as I think) the faculty to enlarge them by any kind of abstraction.[63]

On the other hand, human *conceptual* thought does endow us with such faculties of abstraction — of generalisation and understanding, which can release us from the 'here-now world'. Through the medium of language it is as though we can, as required, take up our particular experiences of the world and hold them in suspended animation in linguistic form as universals, and release them again as and when required. Whilst they are suspended in linguistic form they exist as abstract classes, *universals*, and not the particulars such as we actually perceive or imagine, as images of real things. The doctrine that universals cannot be real but exist only as mental concepts is called *conceptualism*.[64]

Let us consider again the simple example of the word 'chair', as in the sentence: 'Please pass me a chair'. We can perceive, or imagine, only particular chairs, not 'chairs in general', so what has the speaker got in mind — and what does his friend visualise? It apparently doesn't matter; anything of the class *chair* will do. It is undefined. How many legs — three, four? (A rocking chair has none). Made of wood, steel, or aluminium? With or without arms? All are of the general class *chair*, but the class itself cannot be perceived or visualised, only particular chairs may be, for the class, the 'universal', is wholly abstract. It has no physical existence. It could be said that anyone who understands the concept *chair* understands what a chair *is* — it is anything that serves the purpose of a chair to his satisfaction; it is what he feels a chair is like.

Mortimer Adler[65] refers to a concept as being 'an acquired disposition' — a disposition to regard particular perceived objects as being of a certain kind and to understand the nature of that kind. Concepts then are wholly abstract; they have no physical existence, and so are not directly observable. *Concepts*, together with *understanding* are essentially psychological ideas, introduced to explain human behaviour, especially linguistic and other communicative behaviour.

Man's communicative behaviour, the basis of his existence as a social being, makes the most pressing demands for the introduction of the psychological terms *concept*, and *understanding*, in order to explain it and its unique nature. For it is unique in the sense of operating through human language which enables particulars temporarily to take on the cloak of universals, as concepts, whereas the sign-usage of other creatures is confined to signification of particulars, 'perceptual abstractions'. In this respect human language may be said to be categorically distinct from the sign-usage of other creatures; for, whilst perceptual abstraction may be examined as a neurophysiological process,[66] in physical terms, conceptualisation and understanding cannot be, for they are non-physical and not directly observable. Humans and other creatures all may form perceptual abstractions of objects presented to their senses; that is, they may classify them and discriminate between them. Man himself goes far beyond this in being able in addition to conceptualise and so understand what he has created in conceptual form.[67]

However, human discourse is not restricted to discussion of concrete, perceptible, objects — chairs, tables, doors, etc. — for it includes subject matter which is non-physical, non-perceptible, and far more complex. It can deal with such ideas as, *friendship, justice, beauty, wisdom,* — a host of abstract notions. These are *concepts*, to which there correspond no 'perceptual abstractions', no *particulars*.[68,69]

Thus, for example, we cannot perceive 'justice', but only specific acts which we are disposed to call 'just' or 'unjust'. That is to say we humans have the concept of 'justice'; we not only discriminate between various just and unjust *acts*, but know what this discrimination entails and what 'justice' is like. Through such conceptualisation, language enables us to abstract 'justice' out of all specific acts and so to discuss it, examine its nature, theorise about it. The animals can no doubt also respond significantly differently to 'just' and 'unjust' acts, but it is we human beings who have labelled them as such, not the animals, and who conceive them as involving 'justice' or 'injustice', and understand them to be 'just' or 'unjust'.

There are many other ways whereby human language may be distinguished from the various sign-usages used by the creatures. Thus, for example, it serves an unlimited variety of purposes and is not something that has evolved for some specific purpose.[70] As needs change so may the language accordingly, by change of vocabulary, or syntax, or metaphor, or by introduction of new clichés, etc. Again, human language uses a great deal of metaphor and simile, especially for expressing abstract ideas. With them, words and phrases that are habitually used within one sphere of interest are employed within another in non-habitual ways; it is therefore most important that this fact be recognised by the reader or listener (without any special footnote instructions such as: 'the next 15 words are to be interpreted within the field of botany, or astrology, or what-not. . .')

There are many other differences which render human language not only unique but radically different from sign-usages of the creatures, categorically so; this subject will not be pursued further here.[71]

As observed in Chapter 1, man is 'the maker and user of tools. . .in unlimited variety'. He is distinguished from all other creatures, not so much by his reason as by his *creative, constructional* faculties — at all levels. At the material level his ceaseless drive is to rebuild the physical environment, by inventing, creating, changing — and so tearing down some part of his old one as the price to be paid for his progress. At the social level his drive is to change existing habits and customs, to create new institutions and organisations, and to tell others less fortunate than himself how they ought to live. Above all, at the level of understanding, his drive is to break down old beliefs and to substitute new ones, to create new models of the world, in science as in politics, to continually create new concepts, and through this essentially human activity to build a world that he can feel he can *understand*.

Notes

1. Taken from *The Methodology of the Social Sciences*, Max Weber (translated and edited by E.A. Shils and H.A. Finch), Macmillan Publishing Co. Inc., 1949. Essays written between 1904 and 1917.

2. This point will be taken up in Section 8 of this chapter.

3. See 'Human Communication: Value, Choice and Courage in a World of Chance', E.C. Cherry, in the volume entitled *Uncertain Outcomes*, C.R.Bell (ed.), MTP Press Ltd, Lancaster, England, 1979.

4. See *The Principles of Art*, R.G. Collingwood, Clarendon Press, 1938 (Oxford University Press, 1958).

5. According to Huizinga neither would savages or poets either. The reader will find Chapter 15, 'Symbolism in its Decline', of Huizinga's book contains many examples of the ways in which the medieval mind was dominated by symbolism. See *The Waning of the Middle Ages*, J. Huizinga, Arnold, London, 1924.

6. See *The Individual and the Cosmos in Renaissance Philosophy*, Ernest Cassirer, (especially, Chapter 4, 'The Subject-Object Problem in the Philosophy of the Renaissance'), Harper & Row Inc., New York, 1963. (Original German edition, B.G. Teubner, Leipzig and Berlin, 1927). Also, *The Origins of Subjectivity (an Essay on Descartes)*, H. Caton, Yale University Press, New Haven and London,1973.

7. See *Erasmus and the Age of Reformation*, J. Huizinga, Harper, New York, 1957.

8. Sir William C. Dampier (Ch.1, note 17).

9. Scholasticism, the most characteristic philosophy of medievalism, has been called 'an attempt to rationalise the doctrines of the Church' i.e. to relegate the powers of reason to the authority of God. It was not barren; on the contrary, it was an attempt to establish the authority of faith by *reasoned argument* which, in practical effect, was an unconscious acceptance of the authority of reason. (See the *Encyclopaedia Brittanica*).

10. See *Science and Culture, and other essays*, T.H. Huxley, Macmillan & Co., London, 1881. Specially, Chapter 12, 'The Coming of Age of "The Origin of Species" ', (1880).

11. Sir Wlliam C. Dampier (Ch. 1, note 17).

12. J. Huizinga (note 5).

13. See *The Idea of History*, R.G. Collingwood, Oxford University Press, London, New York, 1946.

14. Medieval scholars had access to some of the writings of Aristotle, if only in translation. (See *Encyclopaedia Britannica*).

15. E. Cassirer (note 6), and H. Caton (ibid).

16. I am indebted to Professor Meredith Thring of Queen Mary College, London, for calling my attention to this quotation.

17. Sir William C. Dampier (Ch. 1, note 17).

18. [In Chapter 4 it was intended to offer a definition of 'society' (social groups) as *people in communication*.]

19. See Section 2 of Chapter 1.

20. Of course, the reverse argument does not apply; any sharp stone that we may find could possibly have been used at some time for cutting, just as any stick might have been used to club someone with. It is the expert's knowledge of the construction of the axe-head, his certainty that it could only have been *constructed*, for specific use, that identifies it as such.

21. R.G. Collingwood (note 13).

22. See *Vico and Herder: Two Studies in the History of Ideas*, Sir Isiah Berlin, The Hogarth Press, London, 1976, and Viking Penguin Inc., New York, 1976. See also R.G. Collingwood (note 13), and the *Encyclopaedia Brittanica*.

23. Sir Edmund Leach (Ch.1, note 1).

24. Quotation from Sir Isiah Berlin (note 22).

25. R.G. Collingwood (note 13).

26. To be precise: the type and degree of anyone's understanding of something is limited by the extent to which he can do this (model it, make representation of it). See the opening paragraphs of Chapter 1.

27. 1976 edition.

28. This is, of course, not a solution to the age-old mind/body problem, which is something quite different and which will be touched upon in Section 5 of this chapter.

29. [This point was to have been argued in Chapter 5.]

30. See Section 3, Chapter 2. Also, Sir William C. Dampier, (Ch.1, note 17), J.B. Bury (Ch.1, note 36).

31. See especially his essay ' "Objectivity" in Social Science and Social Policy' in Max Weber (note 1). See also other works by Max Weber (Ch.1, note 24), (Ch.1, note 27), and by R. Aron (Ch.1, note 11). Also, *Social Science and Social Purpose*, Lord T.S. Simey, (especially Chapter 4, 'The Impact of Weber's Ideas on the Logic of the Social Sciences'). Constable & Co. Ltd, London, 1968.

32. R. Aron (Ch.1, note 11).

33. See the beginning of Section 6 of Chapter 2.

34. See *A History of Experimental Psychology*, E.G. Boring, Appleton-Century-Crofts, Inc., New York, 1950. Also Sir William C. Dampier (Ch.1, note 17).

35. Sociology presents similar problems, for the scientist is himself a creature of his own culture and society.

36. See *The Difference of Man and the Difference it Makes*, Mortimer J. Adler, Holt, Rinehart & Winston, New York, Chicago, San Francisco, 1967.

37. See 'Distributional and Non-Distributional Uncertainty', I.P. Christensen, in the volume edited by C.R. Bell, (note 3).

38. E.C. Cherry (Ch.1, note 78 — 'On Human Communication').

39. [This ambiguity was to have been discussed in Chapter 5.]

40. In its psychological or aesthetic senses *form* is not so very distinct from meaning; it is not simply 'shape' or 'arrangement of parts', but refers to a perceiver's response and appreciation of these, or to the satisfaction that the object gives its user. If the object be man-made its form serves a communicative function, i.e. 'gives it

meaning'. See also the *Concise Oxford English Dictionary.*

41. [This topic was to have been discussed in a later chapter, presumably Chapter 5.]

42. E.C. Cherry (Ch.1, note 78, — 'On Human Communication'); Mortimer J. Adler (note 36).

43. See *The Concept of Mind*, G. Ryle, Hutchinson's University Library, London, New York, 1949.

44. See *A History of Western Philosophy*, Bertrand Russell, Allen & Unwin Ltd, London, 1946. Sir William C. Dampier, (Ch. 1, note 17). See also *Encyclopaedia Brittanica*. [A further reference was made, but no details were supplied other than 'Possible ref. to Boyce Gibson'].

45. One explanation which has been put forward by one of his contemporaries (the Belgian, Arnold Geulincx) is known as the 'Theory of Two Clocks'. If you have two clocks, in perfect synchronism, one showing the hours and the other striking them, then you might imagine that the first one caused the second one to strike. But you would be wrong; they are merely *correlated*, and some external force causes this. To Geulincx, this external, controlling, force was God. See also *Encyclopaedia Brittanica.*

46. Sir William C. Dampier (Ch.1, note 17).

47. See *An Essay Concerning Human Understanding*, John Locke, Dorset Court, England, 1689 — and various subsequent editions.

48. In Section 8 of this chapter.

49. Just as, in physics, 'elementary particles' or 'radio waves' are not themselves directly observable by the senses. They are rather postulates, introduced into the framework of understanding and explanation (i.e. the scientific 'model') of physical phenomena which are observable by the senses.

50. For example, such a device as the electronic engineer's 'noise generator' — which may be thought of as a kind of electronic dice-thrower that partly decides the instant by instant actions of the machines, 'by chance'. To the extent that such a chance element renders the machine structure not fully knowable, so the behaviour of the machine cannot be fully understood — but its likely behaviour may be inferred.

51. In the logical sense only. They are, of course, historically and culturally determined.

52. E.C. Cherry (Ch.1, note 78 — 'On Human Communication').

53. See *Reflections on Language*, N. Chomsky, Temple Smith (Fontana Books), London, 1975.

54. Even the severely handicapped (e.g. profoundly deaf, or deaf-blind) struggle to learn sign-language, often with remarkable fluency among those like them.

55. See 'The Development of the Human Child's Native Language', R. Brown, in the volume edited by A. Silverstein (Ch.2, note 67).

56. Mortimer J. Adler (note 36).

57. See note 56 and J. Locke (note 47).

58. As noted in the previous section, 'recognition' is a misnomer, because machines do not cognise. The process should be called 'discrimination'.

59. See Chapter XI, Book II, Section 5 of J. Locke, (note 47).

60. Locke does not use the word *abstraction* in the sense of 'perceptual abstraction', as we do here (following Adler). He speaks of 'discerning'.

61. We do not need to know the rules of syntax, in the sense of being able to state them. We rather may be said to *conform* to their regularities, by habit.

62. This point takes us back to the opening paragraph of this chapter.

63. See Chapter XI, Book II, Section 11, of J. Locke (note 47).

64. See the *Oxford English Dictionary.*

65. Mortimer J. Adler (note 36).

66. And mimicked by technological processes, such as machine 'pattern recognition', though in severely limited ways. See note 58.

67. The Vico doctrine proposes that man can really understand only what he has made (See Section 4). Seen in this light conceptualisation is the mental constructional process that is essential to all understanding.

68. Mortimer J. Adler (note 36).

69. This point takes us back to the opening paragraphs of this chapter.

70. See the reference to L. Hjelmslev in *Contribution to the Doctrine of Signs*, T.A. Sebeok, Indiana University Press, Bloomington, USA, and the Peter de Riddler Press, Lisse, the Netherlands, 1976. See also *Prolegomena to a Theory of Language*, L. Hjelmslev, translated by F.J. Whitfield, University of Wisconsin Press, Madison, USA, 1961, 1963. Originally published in 1943 in Danish under the title *Omkring Sprogteoriens grundleggelse* and in English in 1953 as *Memoir of the International Journal of American Linguistics*, Indiana University Publications in Anthropology and Linguistics.

71. [But was to have been touched upon again in Chapter 5 — 'when we come to compare human communicative behaviour with that of the creatures and that of machines'.]

POSTSCRIPT

The following two passages were found with the manuscript for Chapter 3. The second was apparently written some time later and may have been the last piece Colin Cherry wrote.

I must add a short, concluding, section bringing the reader's attention to the fact that this book is concerned with the question of 'a Second Industrial Revolution' and with whether this expression has any real meaning.

The current chapter has made some examination of the traditional mind/body problem in order that we may better judge whether or not today's 'information technology' is peculiar, in that it may be said to simulate human mental activity, and whether expressions such as 'machine intelligence' have any real meaning. That is to say, we have been examining the nature of 'information technology' in comparison to the nature of what we know (or even *can* know) about real human brains, in order to see whether there is anything so radically new about this technology that could give us reason for believing that its apparent 'mind-like' operations could alone serve as a source of truly revolutionary influence in economic, industrial life.

Our general conclusion has been that this is not the case. It is rather that, if there be any sense in speaking of 'a Second Industrial Revolution', it is because the new, rapidly developing, 'information technology' represents machinery for communicating and processing data, facts and figures, information, messages. . .and not for manufacture and processing of material objects. Its contribution is to the *social*, organisational, *sharing* element of economic, industrial life and not directly to the (electrical-mechanical-chemical) production processes themselves. There seems to be no more reason for drawing analogies between the actions of 'information technology' and what we are *forced* to accept as being *essentially* human mental powers than there is for comparing wheels to human legs. We have technology, an essential human activity, because it enables us to do things that would otherwise be beyond human powers — and not because it apparently simulates our existing powers in any sense.

However, the story is far from being complete at this stage, and will need to be greatly expanded upon in the following chapters.

Fears are being expressed today, widely. Some may ultimately prove to be quite unfounded. What is certain is that it would be very unwise simply to pick them up, one by one, examine them and accept or reject the validity of any conclusions that we may draw — for the bases of the validity of our arguments may well have good historical reasons for changing in the ensuing interval of time. For fear may either have a rational base or not. If it has, in some cases, can these bases be identified? Or, are there clear reasons for believing that they cannot, in other cases?

PART TWO

MATERIALS FROM THE FILES FOR THE
UNFINISHED CHAPTERS:
NOTES AND FRAGMENTS

INTRODUCTION

The Notes and Fragments which follow have been culled from the files left by Colin Cherry for the unfinished Chapters 4-8 of his book 'The Second Industrial Revolution?'

The files contain a small amount of manuscript material; most of the notes are precisely that — notes made from books or on topics of interest. The material spans several years (to judge from appearances) and it falls into four categories: (a) manuscript passages, either written for some specific section or unused portions taken from the manuscripts of the finished chapters and marked for inclusion at one or several places; (b) notes, often numbered, on books or topics (some seem to be much older and are perhaps from Cherry's lecture files); (c) notes and jottings on scraps of paper, torn pages — in fact on almost anything that could take ink; (d) printed material, sometimes with passages marked, such as newspaper cuttings, photocopies, conference papers, committee papers, journals and magazines.

It seems probable that Colin Cherry did not envisage that anyone would look at the files; many of the notes and papers have the appearance of private memoranda, and within any one file they seem not to have been organised, even thematically. The notes from books or on specific topics are exceptions, they are usually numbered and are written on sheets stapled together. However, this organisation was not considered inviolate — pages stapled together were subsequently torn apart and the separate sheets located in different files. Sheets of paper were torn or cut and reassembled in a different order or with other notes, and thus the originally related parts became completely separated. In addition to this idiosyncratic compilation the notes reveal their private nature in other ways. One such characteristic is style. For example, to the top of a page of manuscript Cherry might staple some notes headed 'Instructions to myself'. Another indication of the purpose of the notes comes from the repetitions. A particular point might be referred to several times in the files and these references would be on scraps of paper, often with different wording or emphasis. But perhaps most significant is the fact that almost without exception none of the material is dated.

As already noted in the main introduction, Cherry freely plundered his notes and files as the chapters evolved. For this reason, as much as the others, it soon was clear from an examination of the files that any attempt to complete the chapters would be quite unrealistic.

The thematic nature of the materials appeared to offer the only basis for their organisation, and even here the lack of sufficient chronological evidence ruled out any attempt to chart the development of Colin Cherry's ideas. Accordingly, I have worked through the notes and arranged those which appeared to be relevant into a thematic scheme which is partly his and partly mine. The possibility of including details from Cherry's book plan(s), as additional structural and unifying material, was considered and reluctantly abandoned. The 'summary of the chapter contents of the book' would have greatly increased the sense of repetitiveness without providing clarifying structure because the book was still evolving (along with the book plan). Furthermore, the version whicn reflects his last overview of the complete book was written either before the second chapter, or very soon after it was begun, and thus fails fairly comprehensively to reflect even the finished chapters.

In his book plans and on the covers of the files Cherry did not use consistently any one set of chapter titles. I have selected titles from the alternatives available and the notes have been organised under these titles. They are:

Chapter 4, 'Communication: the Individual and Society'
Chapter 5, 'Communication: with Persons and with Machines'
Chapter 6, 'Technology and Communication — some
               Existential Views'
Chapter 7, 'Technological Progress and the Puritan Ethic'
Chapter 8, 'Communication and the Third World'

I have added almost nothing. My contributions are shown in italics, enclosed in square brackets. Within any one chapter I could have utilised Cherry's book plan to structure the material. However, the book plan did not seem appropriate; it was out of date and the files are in no sense complete. I have attempted, therefore, to group, order and number the notes in such a way as to provide thematic coherence. Where appropriate, or indicated by Cherry, I have used sub-headings (in heavy type) — drawn mainly from the notes — and for Chapters 4 and 8 I have also provided some section headings. For those chapters where little original manuscript material was left (especially Chapter 7) I have made use of Cherry's notes on books or talks. Whilst this procedure obviously entails selection, and thus the imposition of editorial conceptions, I have endeavoured to use as much material as possible — holding back only where it seemed that repetition would threaten tedium, where brevity would threaten incomprehension, or where the lack of specific context rendered the notes meaningless, vague or disjunctive. Editorial errors are therefore more likely to be those of commission than omission.

The absence of chronological guidance to the development of Cherry's thoughts is unfortunate. Notes and manuscripts reveal that the completed Chapter 3 is quite different from what was planned (and although there is much less evidence this applies in some degree to the other completed chapters as well), as is revealed by both the book plan and the quantity of discarded manuscript. Cherry was working on this chapter when, in the summer of 1979, he became seriously ill. He continued to work on the manuscript during the autumn, both at home and whilst he was in hospital. The last three sections of Chapter 3 were completely rewritten in this period. In addition to some notes which appear to have been written whilst Cherry was at Aspen in the summer of 1979, and which shed some light on the views expressed in the last section of Chapter 3, there is one other clue to the development of his ideas. It appears that when he wrote his chapter plan (summer of 1978?) Cherry had yet to hear of Vico's doctrine concerning the 'Man-made World' (see Chapter 3, Section 4). The evidence for this is straightforward. In the file for Chapter 4 Cherry had placed an annotated copy of a paper by Professor Edmund Leach from the 1977 meeting of the British Association for the Advancement of Science. The paper is entitled 'Men and Machines and Their Interconnections', and on the cover Cherry had written 'Vico. See p.16'. On page 16 we find an emphatic margin symbol and the words 'Hear-Hear!' beside the last sentence of the paragraph:

What I am getting at here is that the feed-back by which human beings react to their environment is creative in that it alters the human living space in an intentional way. But this human creativity has special characteristics. I have already argued that in our apperception of the world out-there we redesign 'reality' to make it fit in with the limitations of human brains, but I am now saying that we then go a step further and try to make reality conform to the characteristics of our internalised mental model.

The effect of this latter process is that we generate in the out-there an artificial world in which we can feel comfortable because we understand it. We understand it precisely because men made it, whereas we can never fully understand the complexities of the natural world because men did not make it.

Beside the next short paragraph is a slighter symbol and a question mark. This paragraph reads:

That is not an original observation. It comes from the 18th-century Italian social historian Giambattista Vico but it continues to be apposite.

In the same file is a copy of a letter from Colin Cherry to Edmund Leach, dated 19 December 1978, referring to the BAAS paper and asking for references to Giambattista Vico 'who I thought was more a philosopher of law than a social historian. Am I right?' 'Certainly the Vico whom I know was concerned with the parallelism between human law and natural laws.'

This evidence that Chapter 3 contains ideas and views which were recent in Colin Cherry's thinking, taken together with the evidence for increasing deviation from his book plan, as he wrote, suggested to me the following approach to the organisation of the notes and fragments. In the sense that one can consider the existing chapters to shift in focus from 'Society' and towards 'The Individual' so it seemed that the way to structure the notes was to follow the reverse path. The notes on hypothesis creation and linguistic communication form a natural link between the material of Chapter 3 and the notes from Chapter 5. The notes which serve this bridging function come from a collection not obviously earmarked for any one chapter but clearly related to both Chapter 3 and the visit to Aspen.

The presentation of Colin Cherry's notes therefore begins with this bridging material, followed by the notes from the file for Chapter 5, dealing with language and linguistic communication. The notes from Chapter 4 come next, followed by the material from the remaining chapters, in original chapter order.

In the set of notes from Chapter 4 the main topic is the relationship between the individual and society. Society is the context for communication, but it is also dependent on communication. The notes on 'Existential Views' (Chapter 6) take up some of the points in the completed chapters and the material from Chapter 4. Here it seems that Cherry wished to explore the idea that technology, and communication technology especially, plays some sort of catalytic role (my words) in the relationship between the group and the individual.

In Chapter 7 Cherry intended to discuss the origins of the Industrial Revolution in the Occident. Whilst intrigued by Weber's arguments and analysis it seems that Cherry did not subscribe to any simplistic view of the significance of Calvinism. He stresses in his notes the need to consider the importance of organisation in the history of industrialisation.

The final set of notes (Chapter 8) relates to communication and the Third World. In addition to notes the file contains several manuscript pages on this topic, including a discarded portion from Chapter 2. Furthermore, I have included some notes from the Chapter 4 file (their origin is indicated in the compilation) where they seem to relate to this topic particularly well. The material is wide ranging and stimulating, and it deals with the relationships between the individual, society and (communication) technology, in the specific context of the Third World. Also discussed is the relationship between developed and developing countries. Cherry was especially concerned about the vital importance of bilateral communication services for industrial and social development.

The foregoing comments do not constitute a summary. They are no more than a brief guide for the reader to the structure which appears to me to be dictated by the 'Notes and Fragments' left by Colin Cherry.

'. . .after all, we cannot all be sitting around all day, thinking up new hypotheses, or nothing would ever get *done*!' *Colin Cherry*, from the end of a discarded version of the last section of Chapter 3.

[*Some notes which appear to have been made while at Aspen during the summer of 1979.*]
For Chapter 3 — when discussing the brain's power of creating hypotheses.

1. Refer to Adler's *What Man has made of Man*, see especially his pp. 32, 33.

2. The brain is creating and testing hypotheses all its working hours. Every perception that we make, (when we perceive something *as* something) means that a hypothesis has been formed in our minds, which we may test by reacting towards the sensory experience *on the assumption* that what we have perceived is an object of a certain class (the hypothesis). Consequently it would seem that the brain's powers of sensing and perceiving specific objects as physical entities do not account for its powers of conceiving them as universals, of understanding them (i.e. of acting towards them in a meaningful sense).

3. (My wording) The brain's powers of perception, of sensing, recognising, etc., are inadequate for *understanding*. Understanding is of a categorically distinct order from sensing. Thus we sense, recognise, perceive, *particulars* (the thing) whilst we understand the *universal* (the class of thing). To understand requires powers of abstraction and creation of universals. All our analytical powers rest upon these higher faculties — for example, when we read we perceive the printed words whilst we may or may not understand their meaning; meaning arises from our powers of abstraction and of creation of universals.

The brain is the organ of *imagination*, but we can imagine only particulars, not universals. (The images which fill our minds are always of particulars). Thus I can call up a picture in my mind of some particular person, but not of society or of the human race. Such universals are the result of higher orders of mental power — powers of abstraction, inference and creation of classes or universals. For this, we must have powers of creating hypotheses.

4. Mine. (Machines which can be made today that will detect and recognise specific objects or stimuli are operating at the sensory level. They sense particulars. They do not possess the higher powers of abstraction, central to the process of understanding, which would require, in addition, abilities to create universals, hypotheses. Adler has argued that the human brain does not possess any special (physical) organ of understanding).

5. See Adler's book *The Difference of Man. . .* p. 155 *et seq.* The above distinction between detection of particulars or perceptual abstraction and conceptualisation sets off Man from animals and machines. Animals do not give any evidence of conceptualisation, although they show perceptual abstraction; but Man must be able to conceptualise when he uses language. Adler's argument is philosophical; I can be content to refer to *conversation*. A remark is seen to be understood by someone only by the *relevance* of their reply (a non-physical test) — not by mere repetition. See the new Chap. of 'On Human Communication'.

[*And from another set of notes in the same style.*]

6. Chapter 3. I list here the distinct characteristics of human behaviour as being *choice, purpose, intent, meaning,* 'and other cognitive activities'. Perhaps I should here stress intent as being the key word used by Adler and by Popper. This matter 'will be raised again in Ch. 5'.

7. Stress again, where dealing with the 'lacuna' that I am not speaking about what the brain *is* or is *not* but rather what is knowable about it. This seems to be in line with Adler, who emphasises at the start of his book that psychological concepts such as *concept, inference, understanding,* are not physical observables — they are ideas that seem necessary in order to understand human behaviour, as opposed to that of animals or machines, especially human speech and conversation.

8. For Chapter 5. It was argued in Chapter 3, Section 8, that the innumerable inter-actions between individual persons which create them into societies and various social groups are essentially non-physical but are of another category, namely symbolic. We are not welded into social groups by physical force, but by countless symbolic acts, above all, those of human speech. No doubt there are some people who believe that, one day, the forces of language may be explained in terms of physics and that 'meaning' will be a term that will fade from the scientific vocabulary, being interpreted by physical laws. However it seems difficult to see how this may be

done, whilst it is also not clear to this writer why the ideal should be pursued of reducing understanding of human communication to a single category of thought. Why does this ideal seem so attractive to some?

The categorical error being made, when attempting to reduce meaningful functions of human language to some purely physical functions may be simply stated by saying that it confuses particulars with universals. Briefly, the words and phrases of human speech act in the way they do, so creating social groups from separate people, by virtue of their being universals (classes); and universals, or classes, of anything at all have no physical existence, so that they are not open to physical explanation.

[*From notes in the file for the fifth chapter. This chapter was to be called 'Communication: with Persons and with Machines'.*]

9. The rules for playing chess are known and a computer could be programmed. Although the rules are simple, the variety of games is astronomical. But, because rules are definable and built into the machine there is nothing absurd in the idea that a chess-player, even a good one (who knows the rules) could not be given a good game, especially if data about likelihoods of moves is fed into the machine from successive games. But this does not make the machine 'intelligent'.

On the other hand, the rules of human language are neither invented nor fully defined because such a language is significant of extralinguistic experience (i.e. 'about the real world' in unlimited abundance). The moves in chess are not. So the idea of having really interesting argument or discussion with a computer *is* absurd.

[*Referring to an article in the* Guardian *newspaper, Wednesday 23 August 1978, on the introduction to British markets of the 'first two-way portable link with computer', intended for use in warehouses, airports, shunting yards and the like, a note reads*:]

10. This is a good example of use of computers in what appears to be a 'conversational mode'. Indeed it does raise a difficulty of definition. The computer responses ('answers') are, however, based upon a language-system and not language. The rules are defined and built into the (man-made) machine. Even so, not only may the computer's responses change the thoughts of the operator, but he, in turn, may decide to change these rules as a consequence, or to change the stored data in the machine. Then, both the operator and the machine will have been changed by the experience. But what is the eventual outcome? The human operator may decide to go off

and apply his new information to some extra-computing task —
such as a planning problem in an airport, or shunting-yard or
warehouse. . .or to any other field previously unconsidered if his
requirements call for it. To do this, the operator may (if not must)
infer the relevance of his new information to such planning tasks,
judge the risks of error *without even knowing the rules by which he
does so*. The other partner in the 'conversation', the computer, does
nothing of the kind. We have yet to see a computer put up a new
hypothesis.

. . .'computer languages are really codes, not languages'. . .we
know the rules of codes, being man-made, but we speak our language without necessarily knowing any rules of grammar.

[*From a note on 'Animal Communication':*]

11. We should distinguish human/animal and animal/animal
'communication'. Peirce would have described either in the language of an external observer.

We can only *infer* what goes on in the minds of either human or
animal from evidence of their outward 'sign' behaviour. It is useless
merely to observe one animal (or person) and to reckon what their
behaviour symbolises; it needs response sign-behaviour. 'Signs
cannot stand in isolation'.

There may be one great difference between animal sign-usage and
human language, that Sebeok points out ('Contribution to the Doctrine of Signs'). I have discussed this, particularly in relation to
Washoe, the chimpanzee. Human language works by a syntax,
which is an *objective* reality to the speaker/listener. Not only can I
speak English but I can speak Nonsense-English (Jabberwocky). I
recognise whether structure is correct or not. We pass to semantics
via syntactics; the animal goes directly to the semantics.

[*From some notes on* Prolegomena to a Theory of Language, *by L.
Hjelmslev.*]

12. Hjelmslev always refers to 'natural' language in the sense of
common 'historical' languages and distinguishes them from 'non-
language'. He argues that linguists are 'forced into spheres which
according to the traditional view are not his' meaning that they
cannot avoid considering 'non-languages' when considering their
field at the epistemological level. He uses the Peircean term 'sign
systems'.

Criticises traditional linguist's view that 'language' is *sound* and
refers to its supplementation *or replacement* by 'gesture', (i.e. we
speak with whole bodies) — also *writing, navy flag codes, deaf*

languages, etc. It is no good arguing whether these signs are derived from speech.

It is therefore wrong to consider writing, gestures, and other signs as appendages to 'natural language'. To regard language as spoken sounds is to make an abstraction. These other signs can even *substitute* for 'natural' spoken expressions. He says that linguists should properly study 'natural languages' yet at the same time be aware of the 'wider horizons' of semiotic.

[*And:*]

13. But what do we mean by a 'natural' language, say French or English? It has as many different forms as there are social groups or 'societies' and even a simple text may be composed of more than one form. Such forms might be *stylistic forms* (verse, prose. . .), *vernaculars*, *regional languages* (dialects, etc.), *slang, jargon. . . archaic, public address*, etc. (these are my words — not a quotation).

[*And a quotation from Hjelmslev:*]

14. 'In practice, a language is a semiotic into which all other semiotics may be translated — both all other languages, and all other conceivable semiotic structures. This translatability rests on the fact that languages, and they alone, are in a position to form any purport whatsoever; in a language, and only in a language, we can 'work over the inexpressible until it is expressed' (Kirkegaard)'.

[*Further notes:*]

15. *Meaning.* When dealing with the theory of meaning refer to it as a *value* which is ignored by physical science. Morris, in his *Foundations of the Theory of Signs* says '*it is well to avoid this term in discussion of signs*; theoretically, it can be dispensed with entirely and should not be incorporated into the language of semiotic'. This is because 'meaning' is ambiguous — may refer to designatum (what sign refers to), denotatum (a designatum which actually exists in reality), and at times to the interpretant. 'It has had such a notorious history'.

16. *The vital importance of language.* Human speech is fundamentally different from all other sounds. It sets us in human relationship; it involves our moral code; it demands 'interpretation' (we search for meaning, not cause). It needs a primary decision in the brain. Experiments show that we recognise a sound as speech within 1/10th second. Stress importance of language in view of widespread belief that telecommunication is increasingly for data etc.

17. (Chapter on Language, etc.). Refer to the increasing 'data-transmission' today — the growing flood of computer data over

our communication links. Some will argue 'data are overtaking speech' or that 'computers are over-taking telecommunication'. This is complete misconception. The mere ratio of *quantities* of traffic is one thing — and these beliefs may be true in that sense; but speech is still of vital importance and will continue to be so. It is also true that speech traffic (telephony) and computer data will be increasingly combined and sent over the same routes; but this is a mere technicality. Why is speech so important?

18. Refer to the *discursive* value of speech. How does language work? Data have *significance* but it is the *meaning* of language that we need to examine, bearing in mind its necessary 'ambiguity', its source of misunderstanding, etc. The value of language does not stem primarily from its logical function — it is 'inexact' in that sense and may be criticised by some mathematicians (Leibnitz — see On Human Communication). Its primary value is its socialising function — it has evolved, to serve *needs*, continually changing needs of societies; to serve people whose experience may be very different, or who have never met, etc.

The coming of the telephone was not just the coming of another technique for 'sending messages'. It brought in all these social values of human speech, together with the possibility of moving about freely. Much discussion, within technological circles, centres on such value questions of data, computers and their influences, and telephony. It may be valuable here to consider human language and how its meaningfulness arises — for this cannot be understood within the field of physics. (Two kinds of causation).

It is perhaps for this reason, that human communication cannot possibly be understood wholly through physics and mathematics, that so many Technologists have shied away from examining the real and ultimate purposes of telephony — leading them to think in terms of 'signals', 'noise', 'spectra' and other physical quantities and to dismiss all else as 'metaphysical'. They need to consider also psychological and sociological levels.

19. *Relations with a Person and with a Machine.* Give argument that the ideal machine is totally unobtrusive — an extension of our bodies that does not intrude, or demand attention (let alone break down). It 'fades away', leaving us to concentrate attention and feelings to our primary task. It does not demand skills that we inadequately possess. (E.g. a piano 'fades away' as a machine, to the concert pianist; or a bicycle is as unobtrusive as a suit of clothes — we wear it). But the ideal partner in conversation does

not. He adapts to our performance. We exist through that social relation to the other — we speak, he replies and interprets. We are resocialised.

[*The notes left for Chapter 4 are extensive. The Chapter was to be called 'Communication: the Individual and Society'. I have organised the notes under headings which seem appropriate, and these sections are presented here in an order which provides for good continuity with the material on language which has been presented above (extracted from the file for Chapter 5).*]

Society = People in Communication

20. Chapter 4, Section 1. *'Society' considered as 'People in Communication'*. Communication (= sharing) is always a social activity. More than this, it is *the* fundamental social activity, whether mediated by speech, gesture, ritual, writing, . . . any shared sign-usage. A social group, of any kind, exists as a recognisable entity by virtue of its people having meaningful *membership* of that group, awareness of sharing ideals, beliefs and attitudes towards the group *as* a group, (1), mediated largely through shared language. In Durkheim's terms, 'society is a force superior to that of individuals', (2), and 'man is himself only in and through society', (1), in a sense analogous to the way that our language takes precedence over what we say — we can speak our minds only to the extent that we have acquired the language.

What is a 'society'? A family? A country? A gang? A social class? The term is all embracing. Each of us can be a member of different social groups at different times of life, or even at different times of day. But, at any moment, we exist as members of that particular group and identify with the others; we feel 'akin' and express our membership with styles of speech, jargon, dress, rituals of many kinds. . .as 'badges' of our membership. That is to say, we are members of that group, and feel as such with the others, because we are sharing many forms of sign usage, in meaningful ways with the others; because we are *communicating* with them. We feel as members of a particular social group (family, gang, profession, social class. . .) only to the extent that we are able to communicate with the others.

It is in this sense that I have elsewhere *defined 'society' as 'people in communication*', (3). Such a definition shifts the interest from sociological argument to the consideration of the nature of human communication itself.

    (1) Durkheim. See Raymond Aron, p. 100.
    (2) Durkheim. See Raymond Aron, p. 65.
    (3) 'On Human Communication'.

21. To be a person, one must 'belong'. Sharing *is* belonging, so language, as our primary shared activity is our primary means of belonging.

22. *The person is the creation of society.* Durkheim's argument that society takes primacy over the individual and creates him in its own image is given in the first chapter of his book *The Rules of Sociological Method*, p. 101.

The relevant passage is quoted in Bierstedt, pp. 91-2.

His argument was counter to Auguste Comte. He said that we must explain social life by social facts and not by psychological facts — 'Society imposes upon the individual ways of thinking, of feeling, and of acting that"it has consecrated with its prestige" and this pressure is the distinctive property of social facts', (from Bierstedt, p. 92).

He also argued that individuals change when they identify with different groups and in a crowd, (Bierstedt, p. 93),. . .'even there the constraints are so great. . .that he is apt to indulge in sentiments and activities that are foreign to those he would express in other circumstances. They may in fact be quite opposed to them, and this once again exhibits the power and the dominance of society'.

23. 'Collective representations, emotions, and tendencies are caused not by certain states of the consciousness of individuals but by the conditions in which the social group in its totality is placed'. (Bierstedt, p. 123).

It seems to me that Durkheim is always considering societies as they are, without going into the questions of revolutions, heresies, genius or creative invention. Nevertheless he would have urged us to look for *social* reasons why these original thinkers did what they did and why their ideas took root. The heretic or the genius is still to be regarded as the creation of his society. The society of his time made his revolutionary acts *possible*.

Communication as Sharing

[The notes left on this topic mostly recapitulate the material of Chapter 1, Section 6. However, some fresh material is presented below, (and some held over for Chapter 8).]

24. 'Two's company, three's none' is the old saying. All communication, whether it be conversation, argument, lecturing, debating. . .is a social affair. We always communicate with another. Even when alone, thinking, you are talking with yourself in the language and symbols of your culture. 'Thinking is also a social activity', as Peirce saw it.

The smallest unit of communication is then the smallest social unit, the pair. Two people, in privacy, may hold a conversation. But if a third person enters the room that conversation may turn into a performance.

25. I defined 'society' as 'people in communication'; *shared* beliefs, values, language. They are a society only to the extent that they can communicate *with satisfaction*.

26a. (1) The question:can I communicate with the Martians, the Ruritanians, teenagers, my dog, and even you, dear reader? is equivalent to the question: what am I conceptually able to share with the Martians, the Ruritanians, teenagers, my dog, and yourself? We can communicate only inasmuch as we can share.

[Cherry cautioned himself here: 'Careful, I have changed my views'. This possibly refers to the sort of difficulty experienced when the meaning of a communication changes as it crosses cultural boundaries, and also to the type of difficulty discussed in the Homo Duplex section (the example of incommunicable pain). However, it is also possible that Cherry became unsatisfied with the uncertainty evoked by the term 'inasmuch'.]

26b. (2) The word 'inasmuch' here is important, for there is no question of, say, your concepts being identical to mine (which is not a testable matter*). It is always a question of degree, of adequacy, of practical outcome. We say that 'we understand' when some criterion of adequacy is satisfied — we always 'understand' anything to a degree that serves our purpose. That is to say, the expression 'I understand' is always to be taken as 'I understand well enough'.

[* A note found in the file for Chapter 5, but clearly intended for Chapter 4, goes as follows:]

27. Sanders Peirce dealt neatly with that old and popular puzzle:
I know what is going on in my own mind — what I feel, what colour
your eyes are, what I am thinking about, etc., but I do not know
what is going on in your mind. Do colours 'look the same to you?'
etc.

He considered what is meant by the word *know*, coming eventually to the conclusion that what you can know about your own
mind is substantially no different from what you can know about
another person's. His epistemology dealt very neatly with the
problem of knowledge by accepting that such questions as I have
just mentioned are pseudo-questions, not real questions at
all — because they are being postulated in the reduced language of
objectivity. He introduced an additional concept and built up his
theory from that. This is the concept of a *sign*. In this way he
overstepped the pseudo-problem of object/subject separation.

26c. (3) Language, then, is not to be criticised on the grounds
that it is 'not logical' (Leibnitz, etc. — see *On Human Communication*). Its efficiency is not assessable on such terms. It is efficient
because (a) it can continually change as history passes and as the
needs of a people change as their world changes, (b) because it does
not lead to a final, logical, absolute 'understanding' (as argued
above), but essentially because it does *not*. For example, a conversation need never end; if the conversants cannot understand one
another, to their satisfaction, the conversation may continue. It may
be elaborated, vocabulary changed, illustrated, enlarged. . .until
better understanding is achieved or agreement not to understand
one another is arrived at. A statement, a description, an explanation
may, in principle, be continued for ever. Conversation only works
because we can always do it better than we actually do. (See *On
Human Communication* p. 333)

26d. (4) There are those who believe that it is meaningful to
speak of communicating with a computer, but this idea may be
criticised on these grounds. What concepts do we share with the
computer? There is no doubt that it may be equipped with vast
numbers of stock replies to questions, perhaps with the rules of
syntax but, nevertheless, the operation of language cannot be
explained without cognition. The question posed to the computer
could be indefinitely continued; there is no logical reason for it to be
finite.

Homo Duplex

[*A section of manuscript originally written for Chapter 3, Section 5, but considered more suitable for Chapter 4 or 5. Footnote 29 of Chapter 3 clearly refers to this chapter.*]

28. My own views have already been expressed in Section 1 of Chapter 3, namely that the subjective and objective are united in experience; that the bifurcation of our experience is not meaningful if expressed as two kinds of existence, but that it is if regarded as two classes of knowledge — that which we find we are able to share socially with others, to our mutual satisfaction (communicable), and that which we cannot (incommunicable); the two are categorically distinct.

[*The note which follows was on a separate sheet and not marked for inclusion at any specific point.*]

29. We can experience a pain, but cannot describe it. We can *say* 'I have a pain in my back' which is communicable, but it does not describe the *experience*. If I know that 'I have a pain' that knowledge is communicable, both to myself and to others.

30. A person is a social being, a creation of his society, of its culture and its language; but, at the same time, he is an individual. Conversely his society is composed of other individuals, like him in many respects, they are individuals of that particular culture and language. The person is both a social being *and* an individual; they are two sides of the coin: *homo duplex*. He may, at one moment act and feel as a member of a social group, conforming to its habits and customs, whilst at other and rarer moments he may stand aside from the group and perhaps criticize it, or deliberately break with its traditions and rules. But the two states are not contradictory or mutually exclusive.

If man is *homo duplex*, then it follows that his knowledge is *scientia duplex*. He has both social, shareable knowledge and a private, incommunicable 'knowledge'; the first is his knowledge as a social being, shareable, and integrating him into his society, whilst the second refers to his private thoughts and musings.

Some readers may protest that his second (private 'knowledge') is not knowledge at all, but mostly vague impressions, half-formed thoughts, day-dreams, words and pictures floating through our minds all day — and they would be right. These impressions, feelings, hunches are not clear thoughts or knowledge until they have been *constructed*, in words or diagrams or other signs; that is, when they have been expressed. This is in line with the doctrine of Vico, discussed earlier (Section 4 of Chapter 3); that is, we only know or understand anything when we have made it. When feelings and hunches have been made into words, pictures or other signs they are immediately crystallised into something that is knowable — both to ourselves and to other people. It is communicable.

However, once thoughts have been formulated into communicable words and signs they too may become public; that is to say all true knowledge is of the first category (public, communicable) whilst the second category (private impressions, feelings) is not strictly 'knowledge' at all, but mental activities that are perhaps, when we concentrate, in the process of being created into knowledge.

For example, during conversation, you do not think out before hand exactly the actual words you are going to say next; you may have a feeling that you want to say something, and you struggle to express yourself. Then when you actually *say* it, you not only tell your partner *but also reveal to yourself what the thought really is*. You have 'constructed' it, in language, or other signs and symbols, so that it becomes knowable to you as well as to your partner.

[*And another note apparently originally intended for Chapter 3:*]

31. *Homo Duplex.*

See Bierstedt, p. 244 *et seq.*

Science and religion are often seen as antagonistic (religion includes morals). Durkheim said that they both come from the same source and that both are directed towards the universal (Weber said that science had means, but not ends, whereas Religions had ends but no means). *Both* science and morals imply that the individual is capable of raising himself above his own peculiar point of view *and* of living an impersonal life (reason is a social fact, not a personal one).

This implies a contradiction whose origin Durkheim says Kant did not explain:- How can it be that the same two apparently contradictory principles can operate upon the same person at the same time? 'Why is he forced to do violence to himself by leaving his individuality, and, inversely, why is the impersonal law obliged to be dissipated by incarnating itself in individuals?'

'All mystery disappears the moment that it is recognised that impersonal reason is only another name given to collective thought'. For this is a collection of people, who see their sociability and its thought; yet each person only exists by so grouping himself.

'The kingdom of ends and impersonal truths can realise itself only by the cooperation of particular wills, and the reason for which these participate in it are the same for which they cooperate. In a word there is something social in all of us. . .'

Durkheim on 'Mechanical' and 'Organic' Solidarity

32. (See both *The Division of Labour* and Bierstedt's book on Durkheim).
His distinction between the two was a legal one. There are two types of punishment of offenders:

(a) Infliction of suffering or loss (penal law) — this corresponds to the 'mechanical' solidarity of a society. (It satisfies society because society is offended by the crime).
(b) Restoration of the *status quo* — corresponds to the 'organic' solidarity of a society. (Civil, commercial, procedural, administrative, constitutional, law).

An action is a crime if it offends the collective conscience. (I would have said this applies more to morals than to crime. Does Durkheim distinguish these? But, by choosing law rather than morals he is choosing something that is objective, observable and so theorisable upon. The opening of Durkheim's book states he is concerned with *morals*. However, on p. 64 of *Division of Labour* he says 'law is the visible symbol of morality'). He said penal law was religious in origin (in his *Elementary Forms of Religious Life*). Restitutive law satisfies society because it makes people conform to the society's ideas and morals. It is this restitutive law that recognises the division of labour.

Societies may then, according to Durkheim, cohere either through the similarities between people or through their differences. He argues that the latter is more poweful because it requires each member to see his dependence upon the others (see * below). In practice, real societies, such as ours, have both forms of solidarity operating (and both forms of law). For some purposes we value our similarities and for others we value our differences.

Bierstedt *does* pour scorn on the idea that there *are* societies which are wholly 'mechanical', as Durkheim said (see p. 50). However, we may surely accept the two ideas as theoretical limits, defining a scale on which societies may be placed — though none reach either end.

He further argues that progress is movement towards the 'organic' end*, *and he does this by referring to both communication and transport* (p. 54 of Bierstedt). He argues that the cause of this movement towards increased division of labour lies in growth of cities, which increases the population density. This brings people closer together, increases their interactions and the division of labour. We would expect our modern telephone service and transportation to continue this process country- and world-wide. But continued division of labour is not inevitable!

This does not contradict the popular view that our increasing specialisation is soon going to produce a race of humans all talking to themselves and understanding nobody else. One reason for believing this is that most of our friendships, our familial relations and acquaintances, our feelings of membership of our society do not result from particularly intense discourse about one's job (people who do so are 'bores') but about a host of matters, domestic, local politics, events of the day, etc., etc.

Secondly, to refer to the *cause* of increasing 'organic' solidarity, or relationship through differences, does not imply that the process necessarily continues linearly, or increasingly, indefinitely into the future. The process may flatten off or other social causes may come into action to counteract Durkheim's law (e.g. increasing unemployment and the approach of Gabor's 'Age of Leisure' in the industrial world which will be increasingly confronting the more 'mechanically solid' developing countries).

[*And on the same topic:*]

33. Durkheim's 'mechanical' solidarity and 'organic' solidarity did not denote two extreme forms of society (e.g. 'primitive' and 'advanced'). Rather, he said that all societies show elements of both — and they both are directed towards the same end, the solidarity of society. Thus we all show mechanical solidarity because there are some universal rules even in industrial societies (e.g. one wife each, we all wear clothes, etc.). But in societies which have reached the level of the division of labour we also support each other — 'division of labour' is not anarchy!

34. Note Durkheim's division into (1) mechanical solidarity and (2) organic solidarity of societies. People interchangeable in the former (p. 22 of Aron) — people 'differ very little, feel, think and value alike. . .' (i.e. 'perfect communication'). This could be said to be the evident division in industrialised communities today, between the 'labour force', with its common objectives, and the management

(specialists, experts, bureaucrats) who do not necessarily communicate well, one with another (e.g. accountants and chief engineers). The 'problem' of industrial management arises to the extent that the two kinds of society exist together, in a common enterprise — but having different goals and values.

35. Durkheim pleaded for the 'professional' institutions, mediating between person and state — see Aron's comments on this.

New meaning may perhaps be given to this today, in several spheres:

(a) the size of industrial combines is too large for comprehension,
(b) organised states now confront the individual (e.g. Income Tax) and are overwhelming,
(c) responsibilities of technology and science cannot be interpreted by governments and vast institutions — there is need for action to be taken by the professional institutions, to which individual members belong and relate in purpose and understanding, with regard to acceptance and teaching of responsibilities and interpretation to governments and the public.

We see more mediating institutions developing today, coming between the individual and the state — consumer councils, unions, advisory bodies, professional institutions. . .and an individual cannot communicate to his advantage with a state. And it is modern communication technologies that have aided the process.

Technology and Morality

36. It is said (Chapter 1 Section 5 that 'technology cannot be a-moral'. Certainly, technology-in-the-metal (the *artefacts*) is a-moral, but I am arguing that it has no meaning (no use, no value) outside its social context. It is dead stuff, having no power whatsoever.

But within its social context the man-machine unity *is* meaningful. It changes the person's powers of action and so cannot be a-moral. Its moral aspects appear in two ways:

(a) Upon the individual himself (an existential point), by virtue of his *possession* of the artefact — it changes his feelings about himself and the world. He must choose whether and how to use it. (*It* has power over *him*).

(b) As seen by others who observe and judge him who possesses the artefact and what he *chooses* to do with it. (E.g. Appearance of a new technology creates a new market, affects peoples desires, forces them to choose. Particularly a moral matter for developing countries who learn about Western technology). (*He* has power over *them*).

Hence it follows that technology has power over the society and the individual. As argued before technology, within a specific social context, is a political matter, not solely a scientific one.

37. Bierstedt (p. 118) refers to *Spencer* as saying that the two primary factors of social phenomena are (a) the external environment and (b) the physical and social constitution of the individual. Bierstedt then argues that if so the former can influence society only through the latter: 'If society is formed, it is in order to permit the individual to express his nature' (p. 120).

In modern terms this might be interpreted as meaning that 'a society develops in ways that are possible within its physical environment' (my words). And it is man's technology which is one primary factor in enabling him to do this. (This does not imply that his environment and technology decide what that course of development shall be — only what is *possible*, i.e. the boundaries). Man can physically exist in almost any environment on earth, or in the heavens, given the protection of his technical powers, as no other animal can — from the South Pole to outer space to the bottom of the oceans. But this does not explain why different societies live in very different ways in the different environments of Nature — neither why they are compelled to nor if not why they choose to live the way they do.

Thus if one day people decide to go and colonise the moon (and I can imagine no possible reason why they should want to) it is unlikely to be the Australian Aborigines.

The people who can choose the environment in which to live are those who possess the power to do so. It is more likely to be the people of the USA or of the USSR, as things go at present, who can be imagined as colonising the moon, simply because it is they who possess the power to do so. But which particular section of these countries would go? By analogy to the early Australian history, it might well be their criminals, dissidents, the nuisances who would be sent there.

To be more serious, it is man's technology, whether primitive or advanced, that enables him to exist in the way he does, in the natural environment in which his society happens to find itself. *Technology serves an adaptive function.* And it is the possession of this technology which offers his society any choice, and it is *choice* which raises the moral aspect of technology; technology does not itself make the choices for society.

Technologics ('tools') therefore, are an essential factor to be reckoned with, when dealing with social questions of the present day, or when speculating about the future. They are a *major* factor, though not the primary determinant. It further follows that futurology is a most hazardous exercise, for few people have ever possessed the powers of insight needed to imagine future inventions. It is an equally hazardous exercise to speculate about the future entirely in political, moral, social-evolutionary terms, without reference to technology.

38. The press, radio, TV, are examples of ways in which Technology exerts its powers over both the individual and society by (a) its possession (b) its use. What is the difference between private ownership and control, and that of government? Both are monopolies and could use it for their specific political ends. I argue that our safeguard lies in its multiple forms of ownership and control — which may not be possible in the poorer countries. If there *is* only one monopolistic control this can be regulated by a diverse governing body representing varieties of institutions, (e.g. BBC). Do the press, TV, etc. control us or not?

Unilateral vs Bilateral Communication

39. *Communication   with   the   past   and   the   future.* It is absolutely essential, when speaking of 'communication;, to distinguish between the two modes — (a) the discursive, conversational, *bilateral mode* (e.g. over the telephone, by correspondence, face-to-face), and (b) the performing, broadcast, disseminating (?), *unilateral mode* (e.g. by radio, TV, the press, etc.).

The two modes are best distinguished by interpreting the word 'meaning', because 'meaning' of messages received unilaterally, as by radio, TV, newspapers, books, etc., means something quite different from 'meaning' in the bilateral, conversational mode.

We certainly act, plan and feel as though we communicate with the past and the future. We make our wills, for interpretation after our death; we send letters, to arrive next week. But these are different; the letter is discursive, and may be used reciprocally, conversationally, so as to clarify ideas, to come to resolutions of agreement or disagreement. All the values of human language are inherent in the conversational mode of communication. The former is non-discursive, and our descendants will make their interpretation of our wishes and we shall not be there to correct or refine these interpretations. For this very reason the highly formalised legal language of Will drafting is essential.

With books too. We do not 'communicate' with the author *discursively*, especially if he is dead. With broadcasting too — we at the receive end can look and listen and perhaps boil with rage and frustration at what we see and hear.

This distinction, unilateral/bilateral is not just an academic quibble over words. It has great practical importance. TV and radio audiences are very conscious of their frustrations as passive receivers. Some brave ones may write letters to the editor, or try to telephone the TV producer in protest. But no amount of 'TV phone-ins', etc., can possibly convert TV broadcasts into conversation, for there are millions of receivers with millions of personal opinions and feelings. A 'phone-in' programme may satisfy for the phoner, but the other millions will watch them as part of the TV performance.

For the same reason, unilateral systems such as radio, television, the press, books, etc., must inevitably enhance the powers of *authority*. The responsibilities of broadcasting are almost frightening and cannot be avoided. It is a matter of political wisdom whether a country creates its own broadcasting policy in such a form that it is 'contained' and seen to be responsible by its population. No broadcasting service, no newspaper, can avoid criticism, whether overt or not; it is authoritarian and must be seen to be so.

Unilateral systems, such as TV, radio and the press require two kinds of authority (a) the authorities who plan, control and operate the system, in accordance with the political philosophy of the country and (b) the authorities who do the broadcasting — the writers, speakers, performers, who are necessarily 'special people'. On the other hand, bilateral communication systems such as the telephone service require only the first kind of authority, namely those who plan, control and operate the system; no authority controls our conversation, for we are not *performers*, (not completely true — the Law may constrain our conversation, by prohibiting obscene or offensive speech over the telephone).

40. *Unilateral/Bilateral modes*

The unilateral systems extend the power of authority and so serve as forces towards what Emile Durkheim called 'mechanical solidarity', in society (people all think, feel the same, and are exchangeable). This extreme lies behind the popular view that we hear so often — of 'people all gawping at the telly' or 'they'll believe anything they read in the newspapers' and, indeed, in that derogatory expression 'mass communication'.

On the other hand the bilateral systems encourage the spread of free discussion, of exchange of views and differentiation and so are a force towards the opposite polarity which Emile Durkheim called 'organic solidarity' in society (people mutually supporting one another by their different occupations and beliefs, able to change with time). For this reason, and others, I argue that the bilateral systems (e.g. telephone service) are a pre-requisite for development, not only in the economic sense, but in the social sense particularly.

[*Some very brief notes on trust, conformity and dissent, and related topics, originally located in this chapter, along with some notes on cross-cultural communication, have been held over for inclusion in the Chapter 8 notes.*]

[*Some notes for Chapter 6, which was to have been called 'Technology and Communication — some Existential Views'.*]

41. Open this chapter with reference to present-day disenchantment with technology in general (and the great desire of people to possess it — the apparent contradiction (see Chapter 1)) and concern over communication (TV etc.).

We have earlier referred to the organisation of people into committees, councils, boards of management. . .many forms of bureaucracy, as being *artefacts* ('machinery of government', etc.). These may equally well be considered as technological artefacts, constructed of people, related in function according to prescribed rules, constitutions or customs. We might well apply the same point of view towards artefacts-in-the-metal but, perhaps unfortunately, they do not always seem to serve the public as the public might like — the opposite can be the case. The word *bureaucracy* (OED 'government by officials') arouses alarm in many breasts; it is they who are seen so often to dominate the public, not vice versa. They may dominate (a) rationally, inasmuch as their functions and values are clearly understood by the public, who may then make valuable use of them, (b) traditionally, inasmuch as people are very accustomed to them and trust them and (c) charismatically, inasmuch, for example, that many people feel that they are all-powerful, remote and awesome and 'not for the likes of us'. For example, some of the institutions of the welfare state are greatly under-used because many people (a) do not know what they are for (rational), (b) cannot break their old habits (traditional), and (c) fear officialdom (charismatic).

Bureaucracies are artefacts, machines, but are made of people, not metal, people with ambition, feelings of power, wills of their own like the public. But it is strange that many people, even today, fear technology-in-the-metal in a way very similar to their fear of bureaucracy — they will speak of 'the machines taking over' or use the term 'this technological age' in a critical sense. Such concern must, inevitably, be aroused whilst technology and industry are changing rapidly — part of the price that we must pay for techno-logical 'progress' is the strain of continual adaptation. As argued before (Chapter 2, Section 4) machines have absolutely no power in themselves, their power lies in the hands of those who use them or even merely possess them. On the other hand, bureaucracies do have power in themselves and they are distinct from other machinery in that one fundamental way; they are also to be more feared for the same reason.

[*And on a different topic:*]

42. Both technology and communication are necessary for man's existence, as man, and to know it, because:

(a) he is tool maker and tool user — and the tools he possesses control his thinkable powers of action and so his feelings about himself, his rights;
(b) communication makes the person a member of his society — he is created that way, thinks and feels by virtue of shared ideas, language, etc.

43. Since man is 'the tool maker and tool user' (i.e. technologist) and since communication is a pre-requisite for his existence, I would argue that we must expect him to continually try to invent new tools for improving his sense of existence through communication — though he may frequently fail.

[*And:*]

44. Human rights are technologically determined in the sense that the technology possessed offers liberties of action and hence of thought and feelings. *Choice* is demanded — to use or to reject — and so technology is a moral matter.

I have called acts of choice 'acts of courage' however slight. Take this up again now and refer to *true communication* as such acts of choice and of courage [*in his chapter plan Cherry used the term 'authentic communication'*]. The one who stands up says 'No!'. They are rare; for most of the time we escape into trivial chatter, clichés and platitudes.

Heidegger referred to *authentic existence.*
[The last sentence of Cherry's book *On Human Communication* reads: 'In Heidegger's words, the essence of Man lies in his awareness of his being; and the being is "authentic" only when he is concerned about himself, about what it is that he cares about, and about his motives for doing so, when stirred by anxieties and conscience, when moved by awareness of the incommunicable, the unshareable.']
[*And on Communication and Transport:*]

45. *Communicare vs Commutare.* They cannot literally substitute for each other. But some of our present goals achieved by transport may be achieved by communication, although their effects upon the person and his feelings may differ.

E.g. in Teleconferencing the other person is not wholly present. What is 'presence'? He is communicating and so is shared — partly with the others in his room. He is only partly with you. But what 'parts' exactly? What is the difference between an image and a personal *presence*?

[*Some notes found in the file for Chapter 6. They are not marked as being destined for the Existential chapter and in fact could have appeared in the collection of notes from the file for Chapter 5. (There is some duplication of the material and some is marked for the 'Existential Section'.)*]

46. *Section dealing with relations to a person and relations to a thing.*

47. (I/thou vs I/it)
(The nexus between ourselves and the objects of our attention).

48. (1) I doubt whether one could be seriously *embarrassed* by a TV image, even though one was conversing with it in, say, a teleconference (at least in privacy). (Remember Sartre on embarrassment — 'Being and Nothingness').

(2) A person who goes to attend a meeting, or who has come to visit you in person, has taken the *trouble* to do so. The more urgent is the matter of the conference or meeting, the more it is necessary that the

trouble be seen to have been taken. I doubt therefore whether teleconferences will be adopted for the most serious decision making, for the act of taking this trouble is highly symbolic.

Teleconferences are more likely to be of value, as an alternative to real meetings (a) when the matter on the agenda is not sufficiently urgent to justify the cost of people's travel and time, or (b) as preliminary meetings having the purpose of organising later and perhaps larger-scale, real meetings, (thereby leading to an *increase* in the number of conferences!), (c) when the people attending come from only two (or very few) locations, such as two branches of a firm — because the cost of administrative time from either would weigh heavily upon the one responsible for making the decision whether or not to send several members of staff to a distant meeting. (3) There is no point in the 'video-telephone' (a) because we do not want to know what our bank manager looks like, etc., etc., (b) because conversation works phenomenally well on conventional telephones, (c) it would be extremely expensive, (d) we frequently telephone to avoid being seen. It is easier to be sharp, or even rude, when not being scrutinised by the other — it is less embarrassing. Finally, (e) suppose that you, yourself, do not wish to be seen for some reason; then you could switch your own face off. Then, immediately, you will be seen by the other to have committed an act of rudeness.

(4) In what particular ways does a TV face differ from the real thing? There are of course obvious differences: (a) a face on the TV screen cannot see you, as in a real encounter and (b) it is not three dimensional, etc., etc. Both of these differences could, in principle, be removed technically; the first by having a two-way 'video-telephone' and the second by so many technical improvements that, ultimately the TV image became 'physically indistinguishable' from the real thing. What would then remain to distinguish them would be your *knowledge* that one was a person and the other was a thing.

This knowledge makes a moral difference. For example, when you watch someone talking or acting on the TV you can be just as attentive to them as to real persons; you may be absorbed and not be in the slightest disturbed by reminding yourself that they are only fleeting pictures. People frequently weep at a film. But if at some moment you don't want to see them any more, or get bored, you can raise your hand, turn the switch. . . and annihilate them, without any moral compunction whatever.

In the case of two-way telephony the situation is rather different. You may *wish* to annihilate them but you cannot. . .Rudeness, as an act, reveals your *desire* to annihilate the other.

There are then two senses in which the word 'know' is being used here:

(a) 'Know' in the intellectual sense, as when deliberately reminding oneself that what you are looking at is a film and that there is no real person there at all — but this fact may easily be forgotten.
(b) 'Knowing' in the sense of immediate impression as when talking to someone on a 'video-telephone', a 'knowing' that you cannot forget.

(5) This distinction touches upon a more general point, which is that one's relation to a person in conversation is different from one's relation to a person who is merely being observed. Merely observing another person, who is not looking at oneself is little different from looking at a film or television picture; it is easy to look away, to turn one's back and ignore them, without embarrassment or offence. But one cannot do the same when involved in conversation with another. J.P. Sartre has referred to the mutual *gaze* of the two people as being the dominant factor in this relationship, to which one might add the shared, social, nature of language itself — the pair involved in conversation form a social unity, each giving meaning to the speech of the other and each existing as a conscious, feeling person by virtue of their spoken remarks being given meaning by the replies of the other — a process greatly facilitated by mutual eye-gazes.
[*And:*]

49. More serious is the fact that our relationship to another person, in the flesh, is quite different from that to a television image, so that the responsibility of decision making may be more doubtful in teleconferences. One's relation to a television picture is a relation to a thing; if I don't like the face on the screen, I can switch off — and 'kill' it, with no moral compunction whatever.

This may be true of the picture on a domestic TV receiver — but if you are *talking* with that image, then some aspects of your relationship are human, but some are not. For instance, if you disliked the face, or felt scrutinized by the other, or if you are one of those people who can clarify the mind better when not in company, you

could switch off the image unknown to the person — but you could not easily turn your back to him in ordinary conversation.
[*Other notes:*]

50. Refer back to Collingwood and inner/outer world separation — first referred to in Chapter 3 on Objectivity.

The importance of mood to communication and interpersonal relations.

51. '*Historical determinism*'. See what I have written in Section 2 of Chapter 1, and Section 2 of Chapter 2. In this chapter I am concerned with the *existential* powers given by the possession of a technology — how its possessors *feel*. I have been anxious to avoid Marxist argument of 'historical determinism'. (See E. Leach's first Cantor Lecture).

52. Perhaps refer to this [? *the discussion of the computer in Section 2 of Chapter 2*] in the existential section — as an example of how the possession of Technology controls our feelings. In this case the feelings of relationship between individual and large organisations (or even the state) are affected. The person's sense of existence changes.

The belief that computers lead to 'personal files' and so threaten us. Law is outdated. But all information about it is recorded anyway already, but *not* in one place. Computers merely collect it.
[*And:*]

53. Need for irrationality. Existential Chapter 6, Section 2.
Tourism as escape from bureaucratic world.
Refer to Turner and Ash *The Golden Hordes.*

In fact, *is* today's highly organised bulk 'packaged tourism' losing the whole point? Far from irrational, such tourism today seems to be submission to a new, highly organised bureaucracy. Is it *holiday*?

The old bathing costume, deck-chair, amusement park, gambling, funny clothes, type of holiday was more a break from rationality of industrial life and its discipline. (Refer forward to chapter on Puritan Ethic). If packaged tourism is so highly organised and planned, the holidaymaker cannot be *choosing* to 'break the rules', to be irrational. ???

[*Some notes for Chapter 7, which was to have been called Technological Progress and the Puritan Ethic.*]

54. Refer back to Chapter 1, Section 4 where I have already referred to the 'knowledge explosion' problem.

What situation exists now at all analogous to that in days of origins of Capitalism? I suggest that whereas the chief characteristic of capitalism, as evolving from Calvinist philosophy, was endless *accumulation* of *wealth** (through trade, industry,. . .principle of *exchange*), the most important characteristic of today's situation is the inevitable endless accumulation of *knowledge* (participation,. . . principle of *sharing*).

*Marx's comment 'Accumulate, accumulate, this is the law and the prophet'. (Aron, p. 223).

[*And:*]

55. (1)Refer back to Chapter 1, ('things seemed to be going wrong') [p. 41] and reference to *duty* at end of page. [Now deleted]. (2)The spirit of capitalism in its early Puritan origins was one of duty to one's calling; it was based upon accumulation and not upon spendthrift, a spirit of sacrifice and obedience to God. This did not last, as people were changed morally and politically by its very worldly success. The process became secularised increasingly, becoming converted into one of service to Mammon.

[*And:*]

56. (See Aron, p. 224). Here he emphasises that Weber did *not* try to explain the economy in terms of religion. Because, once established as a principle, capitalism spread widely around the world, into countries of different religions. He was concerned with the *origins* of capitalism and did not argue that Calvinism was the cause — only that 'men's economic attitudes may be governed by their systems of belief, just as their beliefs may be governed by their economic system'. (i.e. He observed their *correlation*. He was not arguing against Marx).

[*From some notes on Raymond Aron's book (p. 214).*]

57a. *Weber's argument about the origins of Capitalism.*

(1) We should perhaps not speak of *causes* of capitalism, but rather of the correlation between its growth and the religious climate. Weber himself spoke of the climate as *favouring* (not causing) the formation of the capitalist regime.

(2) His thesis rests on three observations:-

(a) Statistical data showing that 'in regions of mixed religion in Germany, Protestants (especially those of certain sects) possessed a disproportionate percentage of the wealth' and commanding positions.

(b) An analysis aiming to show that there is an intellectual and spiritual affinity between the spirit of Protestantism (of a certain type) and that of capitalism.

(c) A study of other religions (uncompleted) to see whether social conditions are favourable or discouraging to the development of Western style capitalism.

(3) Thus he asked whether the religious conception of a certain type (*only* appearing in the West, and once only) determined a particular attitude to work. Has it always been absent elsewhere?
He developed his argument thus (p. 216):-
The Calvinist vision of the world rests on five points:-

(a) 'There exists an absolute, transcendant God who created the world and rules it, but who is incomprehensible, inaccessible to the finite minds of men'.

(b) 'This all-powerful and mysterious God has predestined each of us to salvation or damnation, so that we cannot by our own works alter a divine decree which was made before we were born'.

(c) 'God created the world for his own Glory'.

(d) 'Whether he is to be saved or damned, man is obliged to work for the Glory of God and to create the Kingdom of God on Earth'.

(e) 'Earthly things, human nature, and flesh belong to the order of sin and death, and salvation can come to man only through divine grace'.

This combination of points is unique to Calvinism — it excludes all mysticism (we cannot, with finite minds, communicate with God) and is anti-ritualistic (it supposes a 'natural order of things' and so science is acceptable for study of the world). It favours scientific research and opposes ritualism.

The problem then arises: What can the Calvinist *do* in a world so regarded?
[*From some notes: 'Max Weber on Calvinism.' (From his The Protestant Ethic and the Spirit of Capitalism).*]

58. (3) It was laid down in 'the authoritative words of the Westminster Confession of 1647', and the relevant chapters in it are quoted in full on pp. 99, 100. These seem to be the original source of the elements of Calvinist dogma summarised by Raymond Aron, Vol. 2, on p. 216.

(5) Weber goes on to explain clearly what state of mind this created in the late Calvinists — the feeling of utter 'inner loneliness', help-

lessness, obliged to follow his predestined path. Man existed *for* God and Man cannot be in the least concerned with questioning this. A system of utter obedience and discipline, but *not* to obtain salvation. There was nothing he could do about it. All 'magic' was eliminated, being of no use.

(6) (p. 105) 'It provides a basis for a fundamental antagonism to sensuous culture of all kinds. On the other hand, it forms one of the roots of that disillusioned and pessimistically inclined individualism which can even today be identified in the national characters and institutions of the peoples with a Puritan past. . .'

(7) It produced a sense of individual isolation, loneliness and distrust of one another (p. 106). 'Brotherly love' exists only for the Glory of God.

[*In answer to the question: 'What can the Calvinist* do *in a world so regarded? Cherry's notes continue:*]

57b. He cannot *know* whether he is saved or damned — which is in the end, intolerable. He can only 'seek signs of his election in this world'. Weber suggested certain Calvinist sects sought such signs in worldly success — even economic 'success'. He is 'impelled towards work to overcome his anxiety about his destiny. Work is obedience to God'.

(Note of my own: the word *success* comes from Latin *succedere*, to follow (see OED). It is still used in original sense, as when we say 'he succeeded his father in running the firm'. But it has increasingly become used as a value term, to mean 'to accomplish one's purpose', e.g. the 'successful man', 'he succeeded in his exams', etc.).

(Aron) 'There is an amazing coincidence between certain requirements of Calvinistic and capitalistic logic.' The Protestant Ethic requires the believer to beware of the flesh — asceticism is essential.

But work produces profit, or aims to, which is sinful; capitalism provides the answer — that profit must not be spent, but must be reinvested.

Capitalism, then, is an ideal form of self-denial.

[*Referring to Aron p. 212 Cherry asks:*]

59. *What did Weber mean by Capitalism?*

He has been attacked by some, on the grounds that Capitalism is older than Protestantism (e.g. R.W. Green).

Truly, there was capitalism in Florence in Renaissance times, for example, with merchants and banking. But Weber distinguished between these early forms and what we recognise today as the great industrial and business institutions, based upon intense, organised, bureaucracy, with people identified with jobs, and careers in an ordered hierarchy, striving to 'get on', 'make good' and with States obsessed with increasing the GNP etc..

This is an increasingly rational process, with defined goals. . .such as caused Weber so much concern.

[*From:*]

60. Notes from Max Weber's Essay *The Protestant Ethic and the Spirit of Capitalism*, (Allen & Unwin, London, 1930. Translated by Talcott Parsons, and with a foreword by R.H. Tawney).

(2) 'Capitalism' in general means '. . .great individual undertakings, involving the control of large financial resources, and yielding riches to their masters as a result of speculation, moneylending, commercial enterprise, buccaneering and war. . .is as old as history'. (From foreword by Tawney).

(3) Weber referred only to '. . .an economic system, resting on the organisation of legally free wage earners, for the purpose of pecuniary profit, by the owner of capital or his agents, and setting its stamp on every aspect of society, is a modern phenomenon'. (Foreword)

(4) It involved 'a code of economic conduct and a system of human relations. . .sharply at variance with venerable conventions. . . social ethics. . .law both of the church and most European States'. 'What nerved them (the innovators) to defy tradition?' (Foreword)

(5) Mere greed or 'acquisitive instinct' does not explain why — because this has existed at other times in history.

(6) Weber uses expression '*rational* (economic life)'.

(7) The pioneers 'elbowed their way to success in the teeth of the established artistocracy of land and commerce'. It was 'a change of moral standards'. 'Capitalism was the social counterpart of Calvinist theology'. (Foreword, p. 2). The social conditions of England made their struggle more fruitful there than elsewhere in Europe — because the class system was long based on wealth, not juristic status.

(8) Weber's central idea of '*a calling*' (Beruf). The Calvinist did not accept medieval idea of each man's place being decided by Heaven; rather that each was responsible for pursuing his path with energy and devotion, as his duty to God. 'Progress' based on 'diligence, thrift, sobriety, prudence'; virtues common to the religions and the commercial goal. (Foreword, p. 2).

(9) The activities of Calvinists and conservatism of Catholics were

noted by many, as a contrast, in 17th century. (Foreword, p. 6).

(10) Other forces than Calvinism were at work to produce the break from the old tradition — the many effects of the Renaissance (including growth of science and rational thought?) etc. (Foreword, p. 8).

(11) It was later Calvinism (not Calvin himself) that was the greatest influence, in 17th century, giving rise to what Weber called 'the Spirit of Capitalism'. (der Geist des Kapitalismus). (Foreword, p. 10).

The following notes are from Weber's essay:-

(12) Only in West has science developed in a sustained, ordered, organised, way. Elsewhere, India, China, Babylon, Egypt it was empirical observation only. (Introduction, p. 13).

(13) *Method* was lacking elsewhere — in science, political thought, jurisprudence, music, architecture, organised press, education. . . *method* has developed in rational, systematic, ways only in Western culture. Also true of government (the State). (Introduction, p. 14).

(14) The pursuit of gain, acquisition. . .has been universal but 'capitalism' is more than this and appears only in the Occident. (Introduction, p. 17).

(15) He defines 'capitalist economic action' as a rational pursuit, systematic utilization of capital or goods or services for production of money profit.

(I have argued elsewhere that it was the book-keeping of the great estates which contributed to the ordered and systematic growth of 18th & 19th century industry. The balance sheet controls.)

Some such capitalisms have existed in many earlier civilisations, but only in the Occident has 'capitalism (developed) to a quantitative extent. . .in types, forms, and directions which have never existed elsewhere'.

(Remember the wide range of forms today:- Trusts, public corporations, limited companies, nationalised industries,. . .etc.)

In Occident, it has 'developed as nowhere else: the rational capitalistic organization of (formally) free labour'. (Introduction, p. 21). (Stress is on *organisation* — this is so lacking in the poor Orient).

(16) Capitalistic enterprise only possible when business and household are separated and with rational book-keeping — this separates personal and corporate property. (Introduction, p. 22).

(17) He uses word *discipline* (a moral term) as needed to operate organised, systematic, rational enterprises.

(18) Weber opines that 'Western form of capitalism has been, at first sight, strongly influenced by the development of technical possibilities. . .on the peculiarities of modern science. . .mathematics and rational experiment — and vice versa — the '*technical utilization of scientific knowledge*. . .was encouraged by economic considerations, which were extemely favourable to it in the Occident'. (Introduction, p. 24, 25).

(I am arguing too that, in particular, communication technology, from telephones to computers, has been vital for offering us powers of *organisation*, of creating and sustaining rational systems of operation — from local to inter-continental scales of industry and commerce. It all started with book-keeping).

(19) He parallels this value of technology with those of law and administration. . .all are rational. (Introduction, p. 25).

[*Further notes on Aron's book:*]

   61. *Weber's meaning of 'bureaucracy'.*

(1) There have been bureaucracies in all past states — Egyptian, New Kingdom, Roman Empire, Chinese Empire, RC Church, European States. . .

(2) Bureaucracy, in Weber's sense has following traits:-

(a) Permanent organisations involving cooperation in organised fashion between many individuals.

(b) These individuals have specialised functions, ('jobs').

(c) Such functions are detached from his personal life (e.g. home, family) and largely from his personality. People are largely 'anonymous executants'. 'Jobs' are impersonal; they exist when one person leaves and another replaces him.

(d) The remunerations of these persons (i.e. 'jobs'), or rewards, are fixed according to rules — the bureaucracy must have its own resources to enable it to maintain the whole enterprise.

(3) Weber differs from Marx, because he argues that the 'bureaucratic rationalisation must continue no matter who owns the means of production'. It is not a class theory. Weber realised this (p. 214).

(4) I should add something here about the great contribution of communication technology to this rationalisation process, by virtue of its potential for *organisation* (telephone service, computers, remote control. . .etc.). Both technology *and* communication are, as emphasised before, not only essential to the maintenance and growth of our great 'capitalist' enterprises, but their very existence

directs our thoughts and desires to accelerating this process ('growth').

(5) Once the system is established, it serves to *satisfy* certain primary desires, moral drives, of individuals operating it. It seems to be the natural order of things.

Weber was asking why should it ever have started, not why does it continue? What explains its *origins*? What primary *motivation* existed? He argued it must have lain in their 'world view', their primary beliefs and faiths. . .in other words, in the religious climate.

[*Another note in the file reads as follows:*]

62. Criticism of Protestant Ethic as an adequate explanation of development of science in England (?). See R.K. Merton, 'Science, Technology and Society in Seventeenth-Century England', *Osiris IV* (Belgium, 1938) 360-632. Curtis and Petras refer to this on p. 32 of their *The Sociology of Knowledge: a Reader*, (Gerald Duckworth & Co. Ltd., London, 1970), as follows:-

'This study considers Weber's earlier hypotheses regarding the relationship between religious ideas and the development of science. Through comprehensive historical research, Merton demonstrates connections between several cultural and social variables, on the one hand, and the emergence of systematic science, on the other. The Protestant Ethic, cultural values, economic factors, the growth of population, and changes in military organisation are all described as related to the development of science in England'.

[*And a note on* Technics and Civilisation *by Lewis Mumford reads:*]

63. The clock 'helped to give human enterprise the regular collective beat and rhythm of the machine; for the clock is not merely a means of keeping track of the hours, but of synchronising the actions of men'. It first appeared in the Benedictine monasteries for regulation of the daily round of activities and duties, prayers and devotions. He wonders whether this was not the earliest beginnings of capitalist work regulation. (p. 14)

[*Chapter 8 was to have been called 'Communication and the Third World'. In addition to a quantity of notes the file for this chapter contains much incidental material — reports, newspaper cuttings, magazines, articles and so on. I have grouped the notes and given these groups headings. I have included some notes held over from Chapter 4.*]

Industrialisation and Development

64. *Chapter 8 (Opening).*
'Development' within the Third World countries is a gigantic subject, which is continually being brought to our attentions, which arouses endless debate and controversy. 'Closing the gap' as it is politely called. It is a principal concern of Unesco, of other UN agencies and of many national and international agencies. In this chapter we shall do no more than examine some aspects of our twin subject — communication and technology — in the hope of clarifying some arguments and of helping to assess the values that the technology of communication may have to offer to the processes of development.

Since its origin, Unesco has been concerned with problems of communication, although it is fair criticism to say that virtually all its attention has been directed to unilateral services (radio, books, newspapers, TV, etc.. . .*broadcast* or *disseminating* services). Such attention has steadily increased, with growing realisation of the importance of communication both to national development and to international relations; since about 1950 Unesco has become increasingly concerned with the fact that the bulk of the world's printing presses, libraries, radio transmitters, film distributing facilities, TV programme production. . .and all other technology of *unilateral* communication lie within the powers of the richer countries. Briefly, it is the industrialised countries that have the biggest megaphone. The concern of Unesco and others may then perhaps be summarised by the question: 'Does this localisation of sources of information and of powers to disseminate it mitigate against the interests of the poorer countries; on the assumption that it does, what can be done about the situation in order to achieve a more 'free balanced flow of information'?

We shall not pretend to answer this question here, far from it; we shall merely aim to clarify some aspects of it. We shall argue that all unilateral services, such as radio, TV, the press, must inherently be 'authoritarian' in some sense or other, and that the problems are ones of responsibility; also, that unilateral services are, strictly speaking, not based upon sharing and are not 'communication' at all but 'dissemination'; (also, that unilateral services need two distinct types of authority for their operation, with distinct responsibilities, (see Chapter 2, Section 7)). Again, we shall argue that the basic problems of development are those of organisation rather than of technology; further, that *bilateral* communication services are pre-requisites for increasing the scale and complexity of organisations needed for development — although they are referred to far less frequently in public debate about development than are the unilateral. It is only the unilateral services that are given the insulting name 'mass-communication' (radio, TV, the press, etc.,) and it is these that scare people — not surprisingly. Thus telephones (bilateral) seem to annoy people when they don't work but television when it *does*.

[And:]

65. The various economic institutions of this world have evolved over the centuries upon the principle of *exchange* — either of barter, or trade or plunder — in competition for the finite material resources of the earth. If we are to make any sense of the idea of a 'Second Industrial Revolution', based upon information and the power derived from it, can we expect these same institutions readily to change into forms based upon the principle of *sharing*? Surely, the whole economic theory of information must be radically different from that of material resources and commodities? This is a most serious question and there are two reasons for raising it.

(a) Information is, inherently, not a finite resource whereas materials and goods are.

(b) Information cannot be bought or sold (i.e. exchanged for money); you cannot even give it away. It can only be shared.

Unfortunately the word 'share' may have an air of benevolence about it, but we are not here using the word in the sense of sharing my house with you, or my money, or the potatoes in my garden. Sharing of information can be either benevolent, neutral, or malevolent (a simple example of the last is blackmail).

I cannot presume to say what changes will come about in the economic institutions of countries, or internationally, as political realisation grows that our powers of sharing (benevolent or malevolent) rapidly increase through the use of information technology, whilst our powers of exchange may steadily tail off as economic growth rates are forced to reduce or stop, through the finiteness of the world's material resources (coming largely from the Third World anyway). But it may be safe to say that these changes of economic principle will not be confined to the so-called 'advanced' industrialised, countries, as seems so often to be assumed, merely because it is these countries (mainly the USA and Europe) which can manufacture the technology.

Indeed there is considerable evidence of such changes having come about already, since World War II; e.g. there is the immense growth in number and scale of the international organisations (now some 4,000 of them) including those concerned with economic affairs; there is the growing voice of the Third World countries in UN and other international debate; within the more fortunate countries there is growing acceptance of the justice of social responsibility for individual welfare; there is the growing pressure among trade unions for 'participation' in the control of industry; endless examples could be cited of the changes being brought about by spread of knowledge, including knowledge of each other.

Once again, I repeat, 'sharing' can be either benevolent or malevolent; there is no argument intended here that the powers being brought about by the new 'technologies of information' are either good or bad. The word 'sharing' is here used neutrally. The argument is merely that the explosive growth of new 'technologies of information', of which there is no end yet in sight, will offer us vastly increased powers of *organisation* (sharing, social action, communication) which we may adopt in various ways according to our various political wisdoms. If these great social changes come about, nationally and internationally, as many foresee, they can only justify the name 'a Second Industrial Revolution' by virtue of the inevitable conflicts that will arise because our present economic institutions are so largely based upon the principle of exchange, whereas the new powers offered are based upon the principle of sharing.

My plea here, then, is that this vital change of principle (a logical matter) is borne in mind whenever discussion arises about the significance of the new technologies, or whenever images are conjured up in the fertile imaginations of technologists of the year 2000 AD, and all that. That is to say, whenever *valuation* is made of the technologies of information and compared to that of the older technologies of production.

[*And several pages of manuscript with a note stapled to the top:*]

66. This was originally intended for Chapter 2 — but it now seems better for Chapter 8. Notice some of the points have already been discussed in Chapter 2.

Raymond Williams has referred to two principal characteristics of our society, since the end of World War I as being (a) industrialisation and (b) the drive for 'popular democracy.'[1] Industrialisation, steadily and rapidly increasing in the scale and complexity of its organisations and increasingly international in structure, is now no longer confined to the Western World but established in the Oil States and appearing in many countries of the Third World. Second (b) is the drive for 'popular democracy', similarly not confined to the Western countries but also now being witnessed in the Third World, in the sense of a growing pressure for greater autonomy, not only within some of these countries' own borders but also in their national demands for a greater say in the world's affairs and control over their own destinies.

Both these great social movements have been dependent upon the parallel development of our various communication services (though in different ways) — especially the telegraph, telephone and radio broadcasting services.

In the case of the first, *industrialisation*, this rests firmly on its base of communication (especially bilateral communication) and transport.[2] However, these two systems, communication and transport, are not to be confused, as was argued in Chapter 1, Section 6, and Chapter 2, Section 8, although this is only too commonly the case; they are quite distinct for very fundamental reasons. Nevertheless, as complex, highly organised, systems (e.g. airways, railways) the transport services are themselves utterly dependent upon communication for their operation and for their security — indeed, our most modern transport services not only needed telecommunication as a pre-requisite for their organisation and operation,[3] but today use computers and a whole range of 'information technologies'.

It is then not to be wondered at that the various communication services of virtually all the countries of the world should be taken under the wing of government — either directly, by Post Offices or PTTs, or individually by license. Not only are these services more capital intensive than any other, with long amortisation times, but any industrial country is utterly dependent upon them for its economic life and its security. These great institutions which we call PTTs, or Post Offices, or Federal Bureaux of Communication (as in the USA) are so vital and so distinct in their functions that they develop a kind of autonomy, a life of their own.[4] They are distinct in their functions from all other 'productive' institutions, such as those of industry itself; they produce nothing material, but are in control of something abstract — namely, information. Their secure operation is a pre-requisite for an industrial society, for they control the flow of the life-blood of organisation — information.

Sir Edmund Leach has made the observation that of all the inventions that have appeared during the past 200 years of industrialisation those that have introduced new forms of 'communication at a distance' form a somewhat distinct class; they have largely been *radically* new in their effects upon the organisation of social life and not merely improvements upon something that existed before. They have led to radical adjustments in social organisation and acitivity.[5] Those people, or institutions, that possess or have access to this unique class of technology (called here 'information technology') are then very privileged and possess unique powers. Sir Edmund has also commented that, in principle, this has been true of earlier civilisations. Those who have had access to means of communication extending beyond their own cultural boundaries have played a key role in society — he refers to the literati of the Civil Service in China, to the medieval 'clerks in Holy orders' and to the mullahs of Islam.[6]

Turning now to the second characteristic of our society (b) the drive for 'popular democracy', the contribution made by 20th-century communication services has been different; it has not so much been one of organisation as one of stimulation. In particular, it has been the unilateral services, such as radio, that have increased awareness in the Third World of their conditions and instilled a feeling that we, in industrial countries, possess not only the magic powers of productive technology but, perhaps more important, that it is we who control the world's communication networks and the 'flow of information'.[7]

Above all it is the *bilateral* services which are essential to the organisation of industry and of all our other economic institutions (as exampled by the familiar telephone service). Bilateral services facilitate discussion, planning, resolution, enquiry, checking, etc., as opposed to the unilateral services (such as broadcasting) which are strictly not communication services at all, but rather disseminating services (as was argued in Chapter 1, and Chapter 2, Section 7); unilateral services facilitate ordering and instructing, but without themselves being immediately affected by the responses or interpretations of the receivers.[8] The various computer services, data-processing, 'inter-active systems', which are so prominent on the industrial scene today, are essentially bilateral services because they provide information at the request of human operators; they do not proffer it unasked. It is then principally these bilateral services (the post, telephones, Telex, etc.,) which facilitate the elementary processes of organisation, so essential to the political movement: industrialisation.

The Western societies into which telephone services were first introduced (in the 1870s) were already industrialised, though in smaller units of scale and more locally than today.[9] Consequently the demand for these services was rapidly created and grew at an extraordinary pace; the networks expanded very fast, covering and inter-connecting the industrial areas. Personal wealth was also at such a level that the domestic demand for telephones also grew quickly.[10]

The situation in the Third World today is quite different. They need telephone services, not only for their official, international, affairs but also for their internal economic development, if they are to industrialise; the introduction of such services is then handicapped, simply because the countries may not yet have enough industry to support them and their growth, in addition to the fact that there is likely to be very little domestic traffic demand for a long while. These handicaps are reflected in the increased costs of their telephone services, for one of the essential features of long-distance 'trunk' and overseas telephony is that the higher the traffic they carry, the cheaper it becomes. It is a fact that, in periods of inflation, when manufactures and raw materials seem to be rising in cost, telephone and other communication services become increasingly cheaper, (i.e. relative to the value of money). The advantage is always to the richer countries, because of their high traffic demands.[11]

By our export of films, and of our television programmes (perhaps seen in village centres) and by the unfortunate necessity of their using our books for teaching literacy in schools, we have advertised various images of ourselves and of our apparent desires and objectives, that have both increased their awareness and their sense of frustration. Above all, it is our news services that seem to them to prove that we are interested only in our own affairs and economic progress and not in theirs. Most of the world's news agencies are owned, located and operated by the industrial countries, and exist to serve our own interests. Most of the contacts between the common people of the industrial and the Third World countries are, unfortunately yet inevitably, effected by unilateral communication services, such as newspapers, film and radio — and 'unilateral' means 'one-way', as I need not remind my readers. Real understanding between people calls for bilateral communication (the 'conversational mode'); each must be able to check, question, and correct the other. But there are formidable barriers to achieving this for the bulk of Third World populations, who are unlikely to be offered opportunity of discourse with industrialised people, other than through that most questionable means — tourism. The main social encounters between Third World and industrialised people occur at the level of government, UN debates and other official activities and are likely to be so for a very long time. Social encounter scarcely occurs at all between the common people, the working populations, the peasants and those of us who have actually experienced all the stresses of industrial life and who have inherited some of the unpleasant consequences of the Industrial Revolution as well as receiving its economic rewards. And bilateral communication technology is unlikely to relieve this situation directly; peasants have rare opportunity to discuss with, say, Detroit factory workers, by over-seas telephone. Their views of life in industrial society, such as they may receive through our films or TV, in village centres where these exist, or by hearing from their 'leaders' over transistor sets are likely to be somewhat rosy. Above all, they cannot fail to see our abundance of *things*, having amazing and desirable powers — the outward and visible signs of our technological world. But they will receive little, if any, impression of the vast and complex organisation of the industries and other institutions of modern economic life needed as a pre-requisite for their production, operation and maintenance, nor of the great social problems to be faced if they are to create this industrial organisation out of their existing society. Such awareness will be confined to their 'leaders', to those who have travelled to industrialised countries, perhaps been educated there, and who meet their kind officially at international conferences, of the UN or as representatives of trade delegations, etc.

Notes

1. Williams R., *Culture and Society, 1780-1950*, Chatto & Windus, London, 1958.

2. Leach, Sir Edmund, 'The Study of Man in Relation to Science and Technology', (Two Cantor Lectures). No.1 'Technological Progress and Cultural Variety', *Journal of the Royal Society of Arts*, June 1973, pp. 421-31.

3. Cherry, E.C., *World Communication: Threat or Promise?*, (1971, Revised 1978), John Wiley & Sons, Chichester, UK and New York.

4. Leach. See note 2.

5. Ibid.
6. Ibid.
7. *Unesco Chronicle*, May-June 1978, Vol. 4, (3). p. 130.
8. See Chapter 2, Section 7.
9. de Sola Pool, I., (Ed.) *The Social Impact of the Telephone*, MIT Press, Cambridge, Mass. and London, UK, 1977.
10. Cherry. See note 3.
11. Ibid.

Unilateral vs Bilateral Systems and their Values
[*notes from Chapter 4.*]

67. Unilateral encourage authority, etc., — centralisation. Bilateral permit movement, etc., — decentralisation. Communication may encourage *both* centralisation and decentralisation.
[*And this was headed: 'Refer again to following point in Chapter on Development'.*]

68. The unilateral systems extend the power of authority and so serve as forces towards what Emile Durkheim called 'mechanical solidarity', in society (people all think, feel the same, and are exchangeable). This extreme lies behind the popular view that we hear so often — of 'people all gawping at the telly' or 'they'll believe anything they read in the newspapers' and, indeed, in that derogatory expression 'mass-communication'.

On the other hand the bilateral systems encourage the spread of free discussion, of exchange of views and differentiation and so are a force towards the opposite polarity which Emile Durkheim called 'organic solidarity' in society (people mutually supporting one another by their different occupations and beliefs, able to change with time). For this reason, and others, I argue that the bilateral systems (e.g. telephone service) are pre-requisites for development, not only in the economic sense, but in the social sense particularly.

69. *The Values of Radio for Development.* [*Notes from Chapter 8.*]

'*Society' as 'people in communication*' is a definition I used earlier, it conforms to Durkheim's views concerning '*moral density*' of a community. He says (see Aron p. 32) 'the more communication there is between individuals, the more they work together, the more trade or competition they have with one another, the greater the (moral) density'; 'moral density' he describes as 'intensity of intercourse'.

He continues to argue that moral density, together with physical population density and the size of the community, explains social differentiation (in an argument which parallels Darwin's about survival).

70. In this view, the introduction of radio, TV or newspapers into a country cannot *itself* lead to greater moral density, although thousands or millions in audience. But indirectly they can, by stimulating individuals into common interests for subsequent shared, social intercourse. In developing countries radio can be a powerful force this way, as orators have been in the past. Such power of radio then does not arise from it telling or 'instructive' unilateral power but from its ability to create a shared interest — for discussion, argument, even controversy, but nevertheless *shared*.

Radio, etc. must be 'authoritarian', but this does not mean it must necessarily assume the paternal role of the all-knowing infinite wisdom. It can be a powerful instrument of change, but it is not obliged by its authoritarian nature to be the source of truth.

71. *The concept of trust*, (and 'propaganda'). [*Notes from Chapter 4.*]
Entirely notes on Sir Michael Swann's paper: 'The BBC's External Services under Threat?', *Journal of the Royal Society of Arts*, March 1978, Vol.126, 211ff.
(1) 'Just as telling uncomfortable truths about our way of life makes it certain that comfortable truths will be believed, so also it strengthens belief in what we broadcast about the rest of the world. And conversely, when what we broadcast about the world is demonstrably true, then what we say about ourselves will more readily be believed' p. 216. (This is not a high-tone expression of moral rectitude about trust, but is pragmatic and logical.)
(2) In discussion following this same lecture, Mr Mansell (Managing Director, BBC External Services) said: 'The External Services operate fundamentally on a basis of trust'.
(6) Sir Michael: '. . .if you want to be believed when you are telling truths favourable to your own cause, you must also tell those truths that are *not* favourable to your cause' p. 214.
(7) No-one is obliged to listen to foreign broadcasts. Furthermore it is tedious and may even be dangerous. So '. . .we can assume fairly safely that rather few people actually listen unless they value what they hear' p. 214.
(9) It is vitally important the External Broadcasting should be directed at friendly countries as well as countries which are ideologically or politically hostile. 'As soon as one eliminates one's friends from the exercise, one is no longer susceptible to the acid test

of honesty' because such broadcasting might gradually '. . .be based more on ideological or political considerations than on the truth' p. 215.

[*And:*] [*Notes from Chapter 4.*]

72. Also in connection with *trust*:-

There was an article in the *Guardian* (18th April 1978) which, among other things, referred to Japanese *writing* as being 'ambiguous' and therefore possibly a source of their people's attitudes to *contract* — we in the West regard writing as sacred, as an essential basis of trust in contracts. Perhaps the Japanese do not.

The article refers to this as possible source of the imbalance of their overseas trade.

Other societies may have systems of trust based upon kinship, (this could be *family* in the West, or tribal membership — tribes are 'extended families'). The Japanese appear to need to '. . .be thoroughly acquainted with the person' (friend? colleague?. . .). See also 8.

We all trust what *works* in practice.

(8) This view about Japanese language was confirmed by Mr Yoichi Maeda (of the Hosa Bunka Foundation, Tokyo) when I lunched with him on 26th April in Tokyo. (Mr Maeda, a Japanese, is polylingual and a Professor of French in Tokyo who has lived a large part of his life in Paris and elsewhere in Europe. He is familiar both with Japanese and European cultures).

He said that Japanese *was* ambiguous and they liked to think that way — leaving the other to guess a great deal. In other words they did not have the idea that language should have the ideal of 'specific truth', which we can never know, but should accept this fact that 'truth' is what lies within some area, not precisely pin-pointed.

On the other hand Japanese *can* deal with science, as it can with mathematics, because these use *definitions* — it can handle language-systems as well as any other language can. But law is not a language-system, not an axiomatic system, but requires interpretation.

The French may pride themselves that their language can aim at precision and 'truth' as an ideal and that anything else would be inferior. The Germans have shown less evidence of such feelings, as the English have too.

It is feelings and attitudes with regard to one's language that decide a people's attitudes towards trust — and not deliberate consideration and analysis of the structure of language.

73. *Duty and Desire.*   (*Altruism vs Egotism*). [*Notes from Chapter 4.*]

'Progress' as a self contradiction.

(1) All 'progress' requires immorality.

(2) 'Division of labour' needed for organic solidarity of societies only binds people together if it is *voluntary* — if so, there must be some driving motive or sense of purpose in the people. It could be mere accumulation of wealth?

(3) See notes [*presented below (as 80)*]. In particular, the later paragraphs on aid and the donor/recipient countries.

(4) Altruism vs Egotism. 'Progress' involves a people in a continual struggle which bounces back and forth between these polar extremes. Drives must, to some extent, be egotistical, but they are not 'progressive' unless an element of altruism is held as an ideal. 'Progress' requires people to have certain selfish goals in order to change things — the desire for change must originate in individuals, but the activities must be socially directed to be *progressive*.

(5) One cannot be *wholly* altruistic (because we should be presumably selfish in wishing to be so). Can we be wholly *egotistical*? No; because the self exists through society; one would be concerned about the opinions of others.

(6) Similarly Duty vs Desire.

(7) It is the individual who has the drive and initiates change, but it is society that 'progresses'.

74. *Need for Dissent.* [*Notes from Chapter 8*]

Dissent, to be constructive, needs security. It needs to be accepted as constructive. The society must be so secure that 'dissent' and 'quarrel' are clearly distinguishable.

[*On conformity:*] [*Notes from Chapter 8*]

75. We need both agreement and disagreement for progress, but the thought of disagreement alarms many. It is far, far easier to conform than to disobey, disagree or rebel, for these require courage. To point out the errors of a whole society, to attempt to spread new ideas, to set out on the path of reform may require great heroism. It is not surprising then as C.P. Snow once pointed out, that by far the greater volume of horror and bestiality in the world has been carried out in the name of conformity and how very rare have been major acts of disagreement.

'When you think of the long and gloomy history of man, you will find more hideous crimes have been committed in the name of obedience than have ever been committed in the name of rebellion. . .' C.P. Snow, 'Either-or', *Progressive*, 1961, (Feb.), p. 24.

76. *Conformity is the enemy, not dissent, is more true in the rich than in the poor countries. [Notes from Chapter 8.]*

Unilateral services are forces for conformity, for fashions, new habits, new heroes, and are seen to arouse concern. Bilateral services are not.

However, in the Third World, their problem is essentially one of creating new traditions of organisation to take advantage of new technologies (which have no power by themselves). Unilateral services may have great value there — for the long painful process of nation building.

Unfortunately so many of their unilateral services (especially films and TV) come from Western industrialised sources. The concern here is not about conformity *per se*, but that the conformity might be to a Western model. They themselves must produce the services; 'development' is more a problem of social organisation than of technology — of creating the necessary 'bureaucracies' of an industrial society that are acceptable to their cultures and trusted, which must essentially require destruction of some of their traditions and creation of necessary new ones in forms that do not offend their other traditions. Industrialisation does not require all traditions to be lost; social change, economic 'progress', does not require a total transformation. The trouble has been that so often the rich, industrial, countries have influenced the processes of change in the Third World, in ways that trespass beyond those essential to economic development itself and so to offend many other cultural traditions and to attack their identities.

[*On cultural context:*] [*Notes from Chapter 8.*]

77. *The relative importance of religious background.*

When considering whether and to what extent industrial development may be influenced, even handicapped, in the Third World countries who desire it, one important factor must be borne in mind; namely, the precedent (though not necessarily model) has already long existed in the wealthier Occidental countries. The Puritan background of certain European countries (notably England, Holland and Germany) may well have encouraged the *creation* of the new ways of working and living that Max Weber referred to as 'capitalism', with its necessary organisation, discipline and sense of 'progress', as discussed in the previous chapter, [*see notes from Chapter 7*] but the results now exist for other countries to see. Religious background may be less important for the institution of industrialisation, once conceived, than it was for the creation of the idea.

Nevertheless, it may well influence the changes of mind, of patterns of living, of values and forms of discipline that any form of industrialisation must require. The process of such changes involves far more than literacy and the introduction of technology; the key words are *organisation* and *discipline*, both of which will need to change in form in dramatic ways. For this to be conceivably possible, communication services are vitally needed, both bilateral services as aid for new organisation and unilateral services as aid for education and motivation, that is to say for adoption of new forms of 'discipline'.

There is no suggestion here that organisation and discipline do not already exist; far from it. It is their forms and extents that will need to change, perhaps dramatically. The whole broad change required is essentially an increase in rationality; 'progress', however that word is interpreted, is goal-directed activity, goals are set, plans are made, organisations operate towards that end and are judged by defined criteria. Planned, purposeful, development is a rational process.

78.   Continue with notes on 'Weber's three classes of domination' [*See * below*].

Japan has done it. Why not China?

Max Weber's book emphasises organised rational thinking has appeared throughout history all over Occident — but not elsewhere.

Emotion must precede reason. People must *want* to be rational.

Values of radio for changing feelings and attitudes.

79.* '*Weber's three classes of domination*'.

These were discussed in Chapter 2, Section 6. Perhaps I should refer back to this when discussing Third World problems? (But note that Aron believes, as I do, that Weber has got these slightly muddled — see his p. 242 concerning the non-parallelism of Weber's classes of *action* and *domination*).

    (a) *Rational domination* (law, rules, common sense, awareness of consequences, economics, values. . .)

    (b) *Traditional* (habits, customs, ethics, values, language. . .)

    (c) *Charismatic* (leaders, 'stars', fashion, publicity. . .)

Then (b) is perhaps strongest in Third World if they are nearer to being traditional societies, having little change over centuries. (See notes on *conformity is the enemy, not dissent*). But (c) may be powerful too — as a force for conservatism among poor and powerless people, or as a deliberate force for change on part of 'leaders'. Charisma plays a great part too as a force for the adoption of Western technology merely as 'a sign' of progress. It is the *rational* domination that is so often weak — and this is simply because development is a matter of organisation, not technology only. (Remember argument in Chapter 7) [*see notes*] on the increased domination of rationalism as capitalism developed in Calvinist countries. Organisations, bureaucracies, having specific goals, are 'rational' above all else).

Cross-cultural Communication

[*This section contains material from the notes for Chapter 4.*]
[* See note 73.]
 80. *Communication = sharing.*This sounds very simple; if you wish to communicate with others, in another culture, or of different education, or language, or of other difference, it suggests that all you have to do is to search for what you hold in common. Unfortunately, intercultural communication is far from being so simple, if only because that very search for what is held in common (shared) reveals that there are things not shared and so not communicable. And it is these that can so frequently dominate the situation — in international conferences, in translation of foreign literature, in overseas broadcasting, foreign news reporting and many other cross-cultural situations, it is the different interpretations, ideologies, histories and environments, that can be so dominant. Failure to communicate, so often attributed to bloody-mindedness, perhaps wrongly, is as much a social activity as is communication — for it is the lack and its causes that are shared, and known to be.
 Non-communication *is* communication; that is the apparent dilemma. Human beings, as social creatures, are always 'in communication'; they cannot opt out, however much they may at times wish they could. It is impossible *not* to communicate. It may sometimes achieve mutual understanding, sometimes lead to misunderstanding; sometimes result in agreement, or perhaps disagreement but, whatever the outcome, communication is a necessity of human existence. Even in solitude one is with oneself, a chosen withdrawal, whereas in loneliness, intense loneliness, the enforced breakdown of communication begins to destroy the self. As has so often been said,

suicide is a cry for help. Samaritan telephone lines serve as valuable a purpose for the despairing individual as 'hot lines' do for despairing governments — a re-socialising purpose, when destruction seems to be at hand.

The fact that any attempt to communicate must automatically reveal to the partners their inability to do it adequately is itself a communicative act (sharing). Clearly it is of great importance in our world today, because of the increased international contacts and inter-dependence of nations in their decision making and attitude formations. It is important too in the field of aid programmes; the rich, industrialised 'donor' countries and the economically poorer 'recipient' countries may share a little , but most of all they share this awareness of their difference, their inability to share and so communicate. Is it right that the 'donor' country should itself decide what 'know-how' they think the 'recipient' country needs? Or should the 'recipient' demand of the 'donor' what it feels it would like? But 'donor' and 'recipient' are wrong words; the aid programme, particularly the 'know-how' involved, is essentially a mutual, bilateral, process of communication, a sharing in a common activity, not an I-to-thou process.

81. For Chapter 4 and Chapter 8.

Influence has always been exerted upon the less developed peoples of this world by the more developed — but it has mostly been uninvited and unplanned — invasions, wars, piracy, colonisation, commercial incursions, etc. Today we speak of 'aid programmes' or of 'technological aid', as though the influence had become more altruistic and as though it were now both invited and planned. To a certain extent this is true, but it is only too easy to under-estimate the handicaps, in practice, however well-intentioned we may assume the 'donors' to be.

It is modern telecommunication that renders today's 'aid' programmes conceivable, and that facilitates their planning and execution. At the same time, it is partly due to modern telecommunication and dissemination (unilateral) systems that the present-day needs for aid have become so urgent. Broadly speaking, there are still two forms of influence exerted by the richer upon the poorer countries. First, there are still the unplanned, uninvited influences which today may come from the export of our films, from many of our domestic and overseas broadcasts, from the purely cultural effects of exported technology — an influence which has been called the 'new colonialism', or at its worst I would call it a modern Trojan

Horse. Second, there are influences from planned and invited aid, which can scarcely fail to be a cultural influence of the most potent kind — which is an extension of the ancient traditions of *trading*. [*And:*]

82. The immense variety of languages in the world provide immensely diverse ways of talking about their worlds — their models of reality, as they see it, understand it, talk about it.

83. I have elsewhere referred to a message as being shareable throughout the human race. Be more careful now. The *meaning* may change even though the identical message is passed from person to person. (*The message is not a commodity*). A better example might be *broadcasting*. The *messages* may be shared by unknown millions (*so are not commodities*) even though meanings vary among the people.

84. *Cross-Cultural Communication.* I have argued in an earlier book (*World Communication: Threat or Promise?*) that we can understand other cultures only through the eyes of our own culture — but this is not the whole argument.

Mary Midgely takes the Samurai as an extreme example*; can we understand them when, every time they acquired a new sword they needed to test it out? They did this by slicing in half the first way-farer they met. Apparently they *had* to test it out; it *had* to work or they were *dishonoured*.

Midgely referred to the 'moral isolationist' view, which is that we should never criticise another culture, because we can never understand it. She argued that this is rubbish. If the view is taken, then are other cultures unable to criticise us? Equally are we able to praise them, or they us?

Again, we *can* learn from strangers, but we must know which ones are worth listening to.

Also — there are many aspects of our own culture that we cannot understand either.

We *do* and *must* make moral judgements of other cultures. (These others then bear upon and change our own culture.) After all, our (e.g. British) culture is an amalgam of very many others, as are other cultures too. I suggest it is interesting to browse through the OED and note the etymology of the words of the English language — they come from almost every country you can think of.

*'Trying out one's new sword', Mary Midgely, *The Listener*, 15th December, 1977, 787-8.

Existential aspects

[*These and all subsequent notes are from Chapter 8.*]

85. *Western Technology seen only Symbolically.*

When dealing with the existential question of how we feel ourselves to be, as dependent upon the technology that we possess, perhaps I should refer to the case of developing countries. They 'see' Western technology symbolically; not functionally, so long as education, literacy and other social institutions do not exist. The elite that gain possession of it will be boosted in their feelings of dominance; the gulf within the country may be widened, between rich and poor, not by virtue of the use of the technology — merely by possession of it. It would not be economic exploitation; more that of a priesthood. [*And:*]

86. The technology that you, in your particular social conditions, happen to possess, and be able to use, deeply affects who you feel yourself to be; what sort of a person, with what expectations and with your particular 'rights'. Human rights are, in this sense, technologically determined.

Of all technologies these remarks are most true of the technologies of communication — for communication is a pre-requisite for social organisation, the base upon which technical, industrial, power rests.

87. The right to *know* and the right to *have* are fundamentally distinct. The latter must deprive the giver but the former does not.

88. When we speak of 'suitable technology' for economic aid, we do not mean that it may be too 'advanced'. It might be better to speak of 'suitable bureaucracy' to accompany the physical equipment. The technology has no meaning whatever, if divorced from its accompanying bureaucracy — and the great problems of development arise in the creation of the bureaucracy, not in the supply of the ironmongery.

Why should the setting up of an appropriate bureaucracy present such overwhelming problems? Obviously, because the people who form this new bureaucracy are people whose history and traditions have been different from those of the present industrial countries and the evolutionary process of development means a great change in these traditions and in the people's values. All 'progress', however we interpret that overworked word, is self-contradictory in this sense, that it requires changes of traditions and of many bases of thought and feeling (of culture, if you wish) that make up the people and their values. And these bases will be what Max Weber called 'the religious basis' of life.

Free and Balanced Flow of Information

89. *Concern about the 'Free Flow of Information', etc., and the vital need for Bilateral Services.*

The concern being expressed by Unesco and by many commentators always arises in connection with the unilateral services TV, film, radio, print. . .). Unesco is concerned wholly with these. The bilateral services (telephones, etc.,) are rarely mentioned in the debate. I have argued elsewhere (*World Communication: Threat or Promise?*) that it is the latter which are wealth producing instruments, because they are essential to modern industrial, economic and other *organised* activities. The unilateral 'media' (as they are called) are not organisational in function, but rather 'educational'.

They are certainly needed and highly valued in the Third World, for this reason, that they have such powers to aid the political processes of change, of education, motivation and sense of nationhood; the bilateral services are different, being of vital importance for aiding organisation of new social institutions in Third World countries — economic, governmental, educational institutions and they are a pre-requisite for any meaningful adoption of modern technology. Their problems of technological development and industrialisation are in the first place problems of organisation.

In the Western, industrialised, countries the bilateral services have long been established and our economic life is organised around them; they are wealth-producing instruments. For example, the number of telephones per 100 population in the economic sphere (offices, bureaux, industries, banks. . .as can be defined by their special 'business tariff') in all advantaged industrial countries is fairly uniform at around about 15. (In the domestic sphere the home telephone is a consumer instrument and their number per 100 population is highly correlated with the country's GNP).

90. *'Free and Balanced Flow'.*

The exact nature of the disadvantage of the 'underprivileged countries' should be examined here. If communication is *sharing* can information be both *free* and *balanced*?

91. The myth of the idea of 'the free and balanced flow of information', beloved of Unesco. What does it mean? If free, can it be

balanced? Communication = sharing; information does not 'flow' each way.

92. Is the expression 'free and balanced flow' of information a contradiction? If it is free (unconstrained) it cannot be balanced, for it starts from a position of serious imbalance stemming from that freedom.

See *The Unesco Courier*, April 1977. 'A World Debate on Information: Flood-tide or Balanced Flow?'

[*And:*]

93. Again, Unesco supports development of copyright law (which restricts 'free flow'). But there is no liberty without constraint of law. 'Free' flow, unconstrained, would violate rights of the information source.

See *Unesco Chronicle*, January-February 1978, Vol.24(1), 34.

94. State here that I have given my reasoned opinion elsewhere* that bilateral communication services are far more important for Third World development; indeed, they are a pre-requisite for organisation of the necessary social institutions as they themselves want them to be.

[*No reference was given. See, however, Chapter 5, Section 2, of* World Communication: Threat or Promise? *where Cherry uses the terms* organisational *and* informational *in place of* bilateral *and* unilateral.]

95. *Why is direct broadcasting seen as a threat? Why does 'free and balanced flow' matter?*

(1) [*Two definitions:*]
Unilateral communication = disseminating power, implying a superiority of one over the other, a domination.
Bilateral communication = organising power and arouses no such concern.

(2) Hence vested interests might obtain control over a weaker country's cultural values or over their political, economic, decision-making processes.

(3) There is conflict between a country's 'sovereign rights' to communicate abroad and the 'free flow' of information.

(4) Communication satellites are a technology much under the control of the richer countries.

(5) The poor countries fear their demands for a new economic order could not make themselves heard nor can their cultural identity be established, whilst the means for unilateral communication are controlled by the richer countries.

(6) *All* unilateral systems raise questions of authority and so of responsibility. Exactly the same arguments can be applied to any country's broadcasting services and their powers over their people. It is a question of *responsibility*. But the world is not a country and has far wider diversity of cultural values, languages, economic conditions, educational levels. . .

(7) Such responsibility *may* well exist; let us hope that it does. Nevertheless, the dominating factor lies in the fact that many of the poorer countries have emerged from colonial experience and there may well be cause for their deep distrust. They may reasonably feel that their progress is in jeopardy.

(8) An International Symposium was held in Tunis in March 1976. They recommended 'cooperation and exchanges between the non-aligned countries in all branches of communication': news agencies, the press, radio, TV, news films, cinema, exhibitions, research, training, etc. They stressed need to produce their own information and to circulate it among themselves.

(9) They urgently need 'to tell the world about their life, their culture and their efforts to achieve development'.

(10) I myself would argue that to 'tell the world' by way of news reports or other wordy material would not be successful. The industrialised world is already over-loaded with words and print — and can't understand most of it anyway. However, exhibitions, films and other *visual* material can have far greater effect upon Western audiences who are universally accustomed to seeing and 'reading' pictures of all kinds. Pictures may be a hazardous way for communicating *to* the Third World countries (as many films, for example, are not seen in the way their producers intended). But pictures may work better upon us than words — at least in awakening awareness of other peoples, their cultures, their problems — we may give them more attention than we would words, for we are saturated with words.

(12) At the Unesco General Conference in Nairobi (in October-November 1976) the Third World countries 'tabled a proposal. . . [which] recommended that efforts be made to create an improved balance in the world flow of information, with the establishment of a vast programme of aid designed to assist the developing countries in extending their information systems'.*

It recommended:-

(1) measures to counteract disparities in news transmission rates.

(2) measures to support regional groupings, news agency pools and national and international unions of journalists.

Unesco Chronicle, January-February 1978, vol. 24(1), 23.

[*Another note reads:*]

96. *Satellites* are mainly for international telephony and are of particular value to the economic sphere. They can also be used for international television broadcasts, by agreement between the broadcasting authorities. Unfortunately, satellites also lend themselves to *direct* broadcasting — sending programmes from one country directly into the homes of another, without any control or intervention on the part of the authorities, and this possibility rightly raises concern.

The concern arises, not so much from the fact that a receptor country's authorities cannot intervene or control what is received, in a paternal way*, but rather from the imbalance of broadcast programme material that is available in the rich and poor countries.

TV is very expensive to produce. Nevertheless India is one of the world's most prolific film producers and the first Third World country to adopt satellite usage for educational programmes.

*We can further argue that, in very poor countries 'freedom of speech' has as little meaning as 'freedom of action'. The starving have no *choice*. Democracy is something that has to be afforded. What we see as 'paternalism' or 'dictatorship' may seem otherwise to people having no choice or hope. (See Richard Hoggart's paper 'Mass Media: a New Colonialism?' The Eighth STC Communication Lecture, 1978, 2.)

References

Adler, M.J. *What Man has made of Man* (Longmans, 1937 New York, Ungar, 1957, London, J. Calder, 1957

——*The Difference of Man and the Difference it Makes*, Holt, Rinehart & Winston, New York, 1967

Aron, R. *Main Currents in Sociological Thought*, vol. 2, Weidenfeld & Nicholson, London 1968

Bierstedt, R. *Emile Durkheim (Life and Thought)*, Weidenfeld & Nicholson, London, 1966, 1969

Cherry, E.C. *On Human Communication*, The MIT Press, USA 1957, Third edition 1978

—— *World Communication: Threat or Promise?* John Wiley & Sons Ltd, 1971, revised 1978

Collingwood, R.G. *The Principles of Art*, Clarendon Press, 1938, Oxford University Press, 1958

Curtis, J.E. and Petras, J.W. (Eds) *The Sociology of Knowledge: a Reader*, G. Duckworth & Co., London, 1970, Praeger, New York and Washington, 1970

Durkheim, E. *The Elementary Forms of the Religious Life*, trsl. by J.W. Swain, George Allen & Unwin Ltd, London, 1st edition 1915, many printings

—— *The Division of Labour in Society*, trsl. by C. Simpson, Macmillan, London, and Free Press, New York, 1933

Green, R.W. (Ed.) *Protestantism and Capitalism (the Weber Thesis and its Critics)*, D.G. Heath & Co., Lexington, Mass., 1959

Hjelmslev, L. *Prolegomena to a Theory of Language*, trsl. by F.J. Whitfield, University of Wisconsin Press, Madison, 1961, 1963

Hoggart, R. 'The Mass Media: a New Colonialism?' The 8th Standard Telephones and Cables Communication Lecture, 15 May 1978, London. Publ. by STC Ltd, 190 Strand, London, WC2

Leach, E. 'The Study of Man in Relation to Science and Technology,' (Two Cantor Lectures), *Journal of the Royal Society of Arts*, London, June 1973

Midgely, M. 'Trying Out One's New Sword,' *The Listener*, 15 December 1977, 787-8

Morris, C.W. 'Foundations of the Theory of Signs,' *International Encyclopedia of Unified Science Series*, vol. 1, no. 2, University of Chicago Press, 1938, 1951

Merton, R.K. 'Science, Technology and Society in Seventeenth-Century England' in *Osiris: Studies in the History and Philosophy of Science*, Saint Catherine Press Ltd, Bruges, Belgium, 1938; with new preface — Howard Fertig, Inc., and Harper & Row, New York, 1970

Mumford, L. *Technics and Civilisation*, Harcourt Brace Jovanovich, New York, and Routledge & Kegan Paul Ltd, 1934

Pool, I. de Sola (Ed.) *The Social Impact of the Telephone*, The MIT Press, Massachusetts and London, 1977

Sartre, J.P. *Being and Nothingness*, trsl. by H.E. Barnes, Methuen, London, 1969

Sebeok, T.A. *Contribution to the Doctrine of Signs*, Indiana University Press, Bloomington, USA and Peter de Ridder Press, Netherlands, 1976

Snow, C.P. 'Either-Or,' *Progressive*, February 1961

Swann, M. 'The BBC's External Services under Threat?' *Journal of the Royal Society of Arts*, March, 1978, vol. 126 211ff

Turner, L. and Ash, J. *The Golden Hordes (International Tourism and the Pleasure Periphery)*, Constable, London, 1975

UNESCO *Chronicle*, January-February 1978, vol. 24(1)

——Ibid., May-June 1978, vol. 24(3)

——*Courier*, April 1977 'A World Debate on Information: Floodtide or Balanced Flow?'

Weber, M. *The Protestant Ethic and the Spirit of Capitalism*, trsl. by Talcott Parsons, Allen & Unwin, London, 1930, Scribner & Sons, New York, 1958

Williams, R. *Culture and Society, 1780-1950*. Chatto & Windus, London, 1958

INDEX